Teaching the Next Generation of Teachers

Teaching the Next Generation of Teachers

Preparing for the Practice of Learning Communities in Secondary School

Rich Waters

ROWMAN & LITTLEFIELD
Lanham • Boulder • New York • London

Published by Rowman & Littlefield
A wholly owned subsidiary of The Rowman & Littlefield Publishing Group, Inc.
4501 Forbes Boulevard, Suite 200, Lanham, Maryland 20706
www.rowman.com

Unit A, Whitacre Mews, 26-34 Stannary Street, London SE11 4AB

Copyright © 2016 by Rich Waters

All rights reserved. No part of this book may be reproduced in any form or by any electronic or mechanical means, including information storage and retrieval systems, without written permission from the publisher, except by a reviewer who may quote passages in a review.

British Library Cataloguing in Publication Information Available

Library of Congress Cataloging-in-Publication Data

ISBN 978-1-4758-2916-7 (cloth : alk. paper) -- ISBN 978-1-4758-2917-4 (pbk. : alk. paper) -- ISBN 978-1-4758-2918-1 (electronic)

∞ ™ The paper used in this publication meets the minimum requirements of American National Standard for Information Sciences Permanence of Paper for Printed Library Materials, ANSI/NISO Z39.48-1992.

Printed in the United States of America

This book is dedicated to all aspiring teachers in secondary school. May they be provided the means to preserve the specialness of teachers.

Contents

Acknowledgements ix

Preface xi

Prologue: The Case for Learning in Communities xvii

Introduction: Students Have Access to Two Perspectives 1

I: Being a Teacher in the Future

1 Developing a Vision: Helping Students Imagine Themselves in a School of the Future 15

2 Your Students' Leadership: It Begins with a New Mindset 19

3 Your Students' Careers: Staying with the Past or Leading into the Future 25

II: Benchmarks in the Evolution of Teaching

4 Teachers Learn and Teach Twenty-First-Century Skills 37

5 Teachers Recognize Quality Levels in Learning 45

6 Teachers Invite Students to Share Their Voices 53

7 Teachers Facilitate Greater Individualization of Study 61

8 Teachers Investigate Students' Learning Engagement 71

9 Teachers Elicit Intrinsic Motivation and "Knowing Myself as a Learner" 79

10 Teachers Stop the Game of School 87

III: Teachers Leading the Evolution of Teaching and Learning

11 The Story of Jane	101
12 Let's Imagine a Twenty-First-Century Secondary School	107
The Action Manual: Your Leadership Now Leads to Your Leadership Later	121
References	137

Acknowledgements

The author is grateful to all his educational and professional contacts for their help along the way. Especially important were those who were willing to take time out of their busy schedules to review the manuscripts that led to this book. I am indebted to Dr. Anthony Pittman, acting Dean of the College of Education at Kean University and Lawrence Fieber, Executive Director of the Center for Future Educators at The College of New Jersey for their encouragement and their insightful feedback from the perspective of higher education.

To Edward Yergalonis, former high school principal and district superintendent for the Rahway Public Schools and pioneer in the PDS movement, I am deeply grateful for his meticulous manuscript review and the ensuing dialogue from the secondary school perspective.

As this was a book about helping students become teachers, it was critical to get high school students to review manuscripts. My deep appreciation goes to Alison Dooley, teacher extraordinaire, for her help in getting the interest of students and arranging for them to review and critique the author's manuscript as well as meet with him to share the student perspective. My gratitude goes to three such students: Michael Akakpo, Alana Peterson, and Rachael Vasquez for the time they took, the care they demonstrated, and important insight they provided.

Preface

The premise of this book is that in the future the work of teachers and the roles they play in schools will change dramatically. This will happen because teachers will work together to make it happen. In fact, it will be the very act of working together that will generate a vision of change and move teachers to reinvent their profession. This book is about the starting point of teachers working together to drive that reinvention: teacher preparation in secondary schools based on the learning community model.

The fact is that the practice of recruiting and inducting prospective teachers in secondary schools is a long-standing practice but one that has grown considerably in recent years. The vast majority of secondary schools across the nation now have some sort of club, class, or program that is intended to recruit and begin the development of the next generation of teachers. Some schools have even more elaborate programs that include regional conferences and membership in large associations such as the Future Teacher Foundation, the College of New Jersey's Tomorrow's Teachers program, or Phi Delta Kappa's Educators Rising.

As the current state of teaching evolves, at some point it will become clear to teachers that making major changes in the practice of our profession will not only be in our best interest as teachers but also in the best interest of our students and our nation as a whole. Current teachers, new teachers, and aspiring teachers will do this as they become increasingly clear about how important they are and affirm the reality of their own expertise. It is an expertise that is not possessed by those who work outside of schools and pretend to advise, direct, and teach those who teach in them.

John Hattie, author of *Visible Learning for Teachers* (2011), explains three significant research findings about the importance of teachers. First, teachers are the single most important variable in the advance of student learning at school. Second, teachers are the variable over which schools have the most control. Their expertise can be developed. Finally, and most important, teachers, working together as evaluators of their impact on student learning, have the single greatest effect on student learning in comparison to all other variables (https://www.youtube.com/watch?v=rzwJXUieD0U).

The work and research of the National Center on Time and Learning underscores this perspective that teachers working in community produce the best outcomes for students. As developed by this organization's publication of *Time and Teaching*, "Research shows that schools with the strongest PLCs [professional learning communities] generate higher student performance. Moreover, this working together reaches its optimum effect when teachers are involved in school design that expands the amount of time they have to work together" (Davis, 2015).

It is, then, this act of teachers working together trying to understand and improve their impact on student learning that drives the positive effects of teachers and drives teacher expertise. This knowledge of the paramount role of teachers in student learning underscores not only the importance of high-quality teacher preparation and education but also the importance of creating a nurturing context for career-long teacher development. It is a context that develops teachers as collaborators in a community of learners, a community that persistently evaluates its effect on student learning as a basis for continuous school improvement.

The purpose of this book is to support teachers of aspiring teachers in secondary schools as they attempt to clarify why the future of teaching must be different and then to set a new direction for teacher development based on this learning community model. This book will provide guidance to teachers as they prompt aspiring teachers to read about, deeply consider, and practice what it means to be a teacher in a learning community. It will be a direction very different from that of traditional teachers.

In that regard, this book looks to help teachers establish a new mind-set in aspiring teachers. It is a mindset that may be stated like this: the future of teaching must be different, and a new generation of teachers must create that different future. The book will then go on to detail how and why teaching needs to become different and how employing the learning community model for teachers stands to greatly enhance teacher learning, student learning, and teacher job satisfaction.

In developing these themes, this book will also assert what some find to be a novel idea. That is, secondary school is actually the best place to begin teacher preparation, even better than in higher education. This formative period in secondary school is uniquely appropriate for creating in aspiring teachers a new vision for the future of teaching. It will be a vision where teachers enjoy higher levels of professionalism as they take control of their own profession and act as integral decision makers in the operation of their schools.

In effect, our aspiring teachers will be asked to stop thinking of teachers as instructional instruments who deliver content in front of classrooms but rather as the designers and creators of learning experiences, and thereby, schools themselves. In focusing on school design, the teachers of the future will conceive of schooling as larger than a classroom or building site and look to educate students by increasingly engaging them in active learning and problem solving in their schools, their communities, and the world.

THIS BOOK IS ABOUT BEING A TEACHER, NOT TACTICS IN TEACHING

It is important for the teacher of aspiring teachers to note that this book is about being and not tactics. Being has to do with you and your students as persons—your natures, your attitudes, your outlooks, and your feelings. It involves a broad view of a teacher's life, both the personal and the vocational. It looks to help teachers help aspiring teachers to understand that who they are as persons will greatly influence their success in and enjoyment of being a teacher.

So throughout this book, teachers will be prompted to ask their students to consider broad strategic questions: What is learning? What is education? What does it mean to be a teacher? What is the purpose of a teacher? As you look to guide your students toward becoming teachers, it is very important for them to consider these basic questions. In fact, these questions will likely overlap some questions each may have about her life: What does it mean for *me* to be a teacher? How will the purpose of my life be fulfilled by becoming a teacher?

In this regard, teachers of aspiring teachers will want to ask students to explore what has happened in their own personal journeys that they believe has led them to want to teach. Students should be asked to explore their own stories for critical moments or experiences that may have made them feel needed in or called to this special profession. Students should be asked to share these moments with you and their classmates.

This initial reflection on how students came to think that they should become teachers would yield its greatest benefits if it led to students starting a Teacher's Journal, where students kept observations and reflections on what it means to be a teacher. Ideally, class time would be set aside so students could share journal readings within their learning community that would become a basis for thinking and reflecting together.

So as this book helps you and your students consider the meaning of being a teacher, the book takes a broad view of life as a teacher. It does not look to explain the specific tactics of a teacher in everyday work. There will be no advice on the best way to take attendance, how to make sure everybody is paying attention, or the best ways to discipline students. You will probably find a variety of teachable moments when these specific tactics might be best discussed.

Instead, this book will help you help students develop an overall view of the meaning and purpose of teaching. When they have started to figure out the overall meaning and purpose of teaching, then it will be much easier for them to decide on and choose the tactics they will use to be great teachers. There are many other fine books on the tactics or science of effective teaching.

WHAT *IS* A TEACHER?

To help you get started in guiding the strategic thinking of your students about their careers, they might be asked to consider these definitions of what a teacher is.

A teacher is

1. someone who stands in front of a class and talks about a special subject.
2. someone who helps others learn.
3. someone who is caring and works to build a caring, learning community.
4. someone who brings out the best in students.
5. someone who designs and creates environments and situations where people learn.
6. someone who helps others learn how to learn and to be self-directed learners.
7. someone who helps others discover their desire to learn and the path it wants to take.
8. someone who loves learning and shares that love with other learners.
9. someone who is a learner and collaborates with other learners.
10. someone who lives a life of learning and brings students into that life.

Having considered all of these descriptions, you should advise your students that there is no one right description. The purpose here is to think about these various perspectives on what a teacher is. They have probably observed that their teachers over the years have exemplified some of these descriptions. It would be good for them to note, however, which of these definitions they found most appealing. That could be an indicator of what each finds attractive about being a teacher or the kind of teacher each wants to become.

DISCUSSION, THEN ACTION

This book advances the idea that realizing the learning community model is the best hope for the future of teaching. Implicit in that model is a sequence. Members of a learning community share perspectives, learn together, make a commitment to goals, and then take action to apply their learning to achieve their goals for continuous school improvement.

As this book is about teacher preparation around the learning community model, it is important to clarify that this book will direct students to practice the learning community model by following this sequence. Thus, in your classroom, their learning community, there should be

1. a lively sharing of perspectives about learning, instruction, and schooling.
2. periods when students design their own learning experiences to answer their own questions about the conditions of schooling and things they need to know to improve the school. Such learning may involve book research, examination of their personal experiences, using technology, conducting surveys, working in the broader community, doing interviews, and more.
3. the development of goals and action plans based on the students' learning.
4. collective action taken to improve their learning community, their school, or their broader community.

Thus, this book will guide students in the practice of a learning community. It envisions a teacher preparation class as an early practical experience. While it has an academic and theoretical side, this book is mostly intended to be a guide to practice. It will ask students in these early formative years to begin to behave as teachers in a learning community. In all of this, your teenagers will begin a career-long commitment to thinking of teachers as designers of learning experiences that transcend classrooms and schools and who act as agents of change for continuous improvement of their learning communities and their schools.

Prologue

The Case for Learning in Communities

The reader may or may not be aware that in the late 1980s and early 1990s there came two very positive developments in the professional lives of teachers and teacher education: professional learning communities (PLCs) and professional development schools (PDSs). Scores of books and articles have been published that have explained the value and function of "learning communities," "communities of practice," and "professional learning communities." PLCs and PDSs are largely derived from this line of research, theory, and writing.

It is notable that much of the rationale for both movements, which developed in the late 1980s and early 1990s, was captured in the 1997 publication *A New Vision for Staff Development* (Sparks & Hirsh, 1997). This work brought together many strands of research that bore on both organizational development and teacher professional development. The work pointed to the need for profound cultural changes in schools and sounded a new day of sorts for teachers as it outlined and explained how teacher learning is correlated with student learning and why we needed a new approach to both.

Both PLCs and PDSs are founded on much of the same research employed by Sparks and Hirsh (1997). That research emphasized the organizational value and the learning value of higher levels of teacher participation and leadership in the design of student learning and teacher learning. In effect, these movements looked to make teacher thinking and creativity central to school operations. Both PDSs and PLCs are about teachers being involved in and leading schools' decision making about learning and schooling.

THE END OF TEACHER ISOLATION AND TOP-DOWN AUTHORITY STRUCTURES

Much of the interest in the learning community concept in the 1990s was in reaction to two interrelated conditions in the traditional practice of teaching. One condition was that teachers usually worked in isolation from one another. Behind the closed doors of their classrooms, each teacher largely did his or her own thing to implement the school's curriculum.

Apart from some common requirements of their position as teachers, teachers did not collaborate on how to improve the practice of teaching. Professional development was most often one-shot presentations where teachers primarily sat and listened to "whims, fads, opportunism, and ideology" that had little relationship to what they did every day (cited by Schmoker, 2015). Remarkably, teachers rarely considered the idea of improving student learning by consulting research for the purpose of collaborating with one another to change any of the traditional practices, structures, or procedures of the school.

The second condition was the top-down command and control authority structure in schools where teachers were often excluded from important decision making about their schools. Decision making was left to school or central office administrators. This structure is a legacy left over from the design of schools like factories from the Industrial Age. People at the top did the thinking. People at the bottom followed directions.

Contrary to the intent of PLCs and PDSs, over recent decades this legacy has been strengthened as the most important decisions for schools came from outside authorities in state capitals or Washington, D.C. This has left many teachers frustrated, feeling as if it was not their job to think and create but rather to just follow orders and implement the decisions of higher authorities. Teachers were often put in the position of implementing decisions that they believed were wrong for their schools and local populations.

THE LEARNING COMMUNITY MODEL PROMISED CHANGE

The advent of the learning community model promised to put an end to teacher isolation and exclusion from decision making. Briefly put, professional learning communities are formed when teachers get together to share perspectives and work together on matters of learning: lesson design, lesson study, evaluation protocols, curriculum development, and/or ad hoc problem solving of all sorts.

A PLC could be in a small group situation where teachers exchange ideas about how social studies and English teachers might work together to teach a

Victorian novel. Or, a PLC could be where teachers have come together to talk about how to insert emotional education into scientific lab work.

PLCs can also be large collectives such as an entire school faculty. In these circumstances, teachers might discuss the standards, goals, and objectives of the school. Such PLCs invite thinking, reflection, imagination, and broad involvement from all members of a school. Most theorists would agree that PLCs were advocated in order to invite not only teacher input but also teacher leadership (DuFour et al., 2006; Schlechty, 2002; Wenger et al., 2002).

The learning community concept acknowledges that the real-world workplace in a school is the actual site of teachers learning to teach. Yes, courses and degrees taken and earned at a college or university have a role, but the most important learning for teachers will come from sharing and learning that is embedded in their everyday work in a school. The concept maintains that if a school operates as a learning community, teacher learning will be propelled to higher levels by the very fact of working together.

If a school does not function as a learning community but rather fosters isolation and exclusion from important decision making, teacher learning will be greatly inhibited or even become negative and lead to teacher disengagement. Recent research by the Gallup organization suggests that teacher disengagement is, in fact, currently at very high levels (Busteed, 2014). There is more to come on teacher disengagement.

The learning community model affirms that the greatest force for a teacher's professional development will come, then, on the job in a learning community where a teacher will likely spend decades developing her craft and career. It will not come from a degree program at a college or university, and it certainly won't come from teaching in isolation or being excluded from important school decision making.

The guiding concept is that in a community of practice all members of a school should come together for collective learning and collective action as a result of that learning. In such communities, teachers are expected to collaborate and act as thinkers, creators, and innovators. Such a scenario acknowledges contemporary organizational theory that sees all members of an organization as agents of change empowered to learn, reflect, and alter the organization for continuous improvement (Deming, 1983; DuFour & Fullan, 2013; Senge, 1990; Senge et al., 2000).

THE COMPELLING LOGIC OF THE LEARNING COMMUNITY

In contrast to working in isolation or being marginalized from decision making, the learning community concept posits that learning is often deeper and develops faster when it is done in community. The idea follows the common saying that "two heads are better than one." In other words, when people are trying to learn together, the sharing of ideas and perspectives and the resulting feedback tends to lead to better thinking and better actions.

You may have noticed in your own experience that when you attempt to explain yourself to others, the very act of explaining helps you understand your own thinking better. At the same time, getting feedback from the people to whom you have tried to explain something also helps refine and push your thinking forward so your ideas become better and better as a result of the process of working as a community. Conversely, listening to the ideas of others and giving feedback also tends to improve everyone's thinking.

This aspect of the learning community model was, of course, very compelling, and in the late 1980s and 1990s both policymakers and local school leaders roundly embraced the concept. Around the nation, the term *learning community* became a buzzword for the latest innovation in schooling. It promised teachers more leadership and much greater influence in their schools, in the design of student learning, and their own learning.

ENDORSED BY NAPDS AND NCATE

It is also notable that the goal of having teachers inducted and developed within communities of learning has also been stipulated as fundamental by two associations that have been primary drivers in teacher education, the National Association of Professional Development Schools and the National Council for Accreditation of Teacher Education (now CAEP). Each has long noted the importance of using the school setting to enhance the clinical basis of teacher education.

Thus, fundamental to the inception of PDSs has been the value of local schools and nearby institutions of higher education forming partnerships to facilitate moving teacher education out of higher education classrooms and into actual schools. In these schools, novice teachers would enter communities of support, inquiry, and practice that provide a concrete basis for conceptualizing effective teaching, observing effective teaching, and being guided in the practice of effective teaching.

Underscoring this commitment to community learning, the NAPDS has, for example, advanced a list of Nine Essentials that guide the association's work and research. These Nine Essentials appear on the inside cover of every issue of the NAPDS's journal, School-University Partnership. Among the Essentials, three make explicit reference to the role of community in teacher learning and development.

> 2. a school-university culture committed to the preparation of future educators that embraces their active engagement in the school community
> 4. a shared commitment to innovative and reflective practice by all participants

7. a structure that allows all participants a forum for ongoing governance, reflection, and collaboration.

Similarly, NCATE has stipulated an emphasis on school-based learning to enhance the clinical component of teacher education. As a result of convening a Blue Ribbon Panel in 2010, NCATE produced a report, *Transforming Teacher Education through Clinical Practice: A National Strategy to Prepare Effective Teachers* (NCATE, 2010). The report provided Design Principles for teacher education, which included
"candidates learn in an interactive learning community" (NCATE, 2010).

The guidance provided by the NAPDS and NCATE are, of course, very consistent with the proposal of this book: to begin teacher preparation in secondary schools under the learning community model. Secondary school is, in fact, a clinical setting where students enjoy access to two perspectives and can employ those perspectives in determining what they, as prospective teachers, need to know in order to achieve the status of being effective teachers. Moreover, they will do this while they learn the practices of a learning community in an actual school.

With that knowledge, they can begin the process of planning their own learning as they anticipate planning the learning of youths who will someday be their students. Most important, such teacher education would capitalize on secondary students' unique access to two perspectives and the opportunity to examine learning at school from both the experience of being a student and the experience of being a teacher. It is an opportunity that should not be wasted.

THE PERSONAL BENEFITS OF THE LEARNING COMMUNITY MODEL

Another aspect of the learning community model was also very compelling. It provided personal benefits to individuals. Along with the benefit of improving the practice of teaching, research into learning communities explained how it addressed the human need for continuous learning and thoughtful, decisive participation in any organization.

Such participation would promise very fulfilling careers to teachers as respected professionals charged with the continuous improvement of their schools. These benefits included:

1. A greater sense of belonging, of being a respected member of a team.
2. A greater sense of ownership of the overall institution and its goals.
3. A greater sense of control over one's work.
4. A greater sense of respect and care from one's peers.

5. A greater sense of being respected as a thinker, designer, and decision maker.
6. A greater sense of professional growth and fulfillment.

These personal benefits have been the subject of many a professional treatise on why teachers should adopt the learning community model for their schools. Under the learning community model, teachers not only stand to improve their clinical practice in helping students learn, they also stand to enjoy much fuller professional lives working in collaboration with their peers. Such higher levels of teacher engagement have high correlation with student engagement and learning (Busteed, 2014).

With the above information in mind, the reader is asked to take a moment to envision how being a member of a real learning community would be experienced. Imagine you and your colleagues discussing some of the hard issues that teachers face and then making decisions that would change your school for the better. That's right, as a result of examining conditions, sharing perspectives, and making decisions, teachers would guide their schools to continuous improvement. How would that feel? How does it compare to having outsiders make the important decisions for your school?

Now, if you find yourself thinking, "Oh, that is pie in the sky" or "That's too simplistic or idealistic," you are cautioned. The fact is that such teacher participation and influence is already happening. More than a decade ago, Senge, Cambron-McCabe, Lucas, Smith, Dutton, and Kleiner advanced the work *Schools That Learn* (2000) and explained the concept of schools as learning organizations where the thinking for schools was done in schools. Most important, they gave many, many examples of such schools and their wonderful outcomes. An updated version of this work was reissued in 2012.

More recently Farris-Berg, Dirkswager, and Junge had their research published in *Trusting Teachers with School Success: What Happens When Teachers Call the Shots*. Their study of teacher-run schools clarifies the many challenges of teacher-run schools and their great promise. It tells the story of many teacher-led schools, their important progress in student learning, and the valuable growth opportunities such schools provide teachers.

Add to this that even the NEA has a Commission on Effective Teachers and Teaching and has charged its members to "craft a new vision of a teaching profession that is led by teachers and ensures teaching effectiveness." The point is this: the evolution of teaching is already in progress. Change has already begun.

TEACHERS HUMANIZING SCHOOLS

In spite of these forces for change, teachers of the future, like teachers now, will be confronted with a professional dilemma. On the one hand, society will be asking schools to show clear evidence of improved learning for all students. As it does now, that will likely mean enhanced efforts to control student learning with more rigid standards, more required subjects, and more standardized testing. This will exacerbate the bureaucratic, factory feel of school for students.

At the same time, teachers will likely want to advance their community goal of humanizing schools so students learn the interpersonal skills they will need to become good people in a good society. Teachers will not want students to think the most important things in schools are the content, the standards, or the tests. *They will want students to know that students are the most important part of school.* This is what communities convey. We already see teachers' desire to humanize schools with their initiation of character education; antibullying programs; peer leadership; peer conflict resolution; active, constructive responding; Penn Resiliency; and other programs. Most important, they are inviting students into the formation of caring learning communities.

All of these programs are an effort to establish a human element at school amid an onslaught of rules, requirements, and regulations that standardize and dehumanize students as individuals. With the forces for the standardization of schooling expanding every day, future teachers will be constantly faced with balancing society's desire for easily quantified proof of improved learning with creating humane conditions for students so they know that their development as empathetic citizens committed to caring in a community is the most important learning they will ever do.

As students form their learning communities this year, they will want to keep in mind how those communities will develop *caring* as the centerpiece of their efforts. What will their learning communities do that will make individuals feel important, included, and cared for?

THE UNREALIZED PROMISE OF THE LEARNING COMMUNITY MODEL

There is a strong likelihood that you have heard the term *learning community* in the course of your academic study or around the school where you work. The learning community concept is often discussed in education textbooks, and many states have endorsed the idea for their schools. If you are very lucky, you may actually work in a school that has real learning communities. The reality, however, is that most teachers do not.

Unfortunately, the learning community concept has gotten more lip service than genuine implementation. This is most often manifested in schools that have pretend learning communities. Because school leaders know that the learning community concept is fashionable, many have been moved to think that any situation in which teachers are sharing ideas or collaborating on common projects means that their schools are operating as learning communities. They are not.

Still other schools have teacher activities that mirror the reality of a learning community, but these activities are occasional, episodic, and not integral to school operations. Teachers do not see that their thinking and decision making exerts any real influence in the school. Mostly, it generates elaborate paperwork that is used as proof of learning communities. From all of this, teachers have a sense of going through the motions because they see very little in terms of substantial change in their schools.

It is in light of these pretend learning communities that it must be made very clear. The incidental or occasional facilitation of teachers talking with one another, collaborating, or even the creation of elaborate documents does not constitute true implementation of the learning community model. A review of the literature makes it clear that a genuine implementation of the learning community model constitutes a major and thoroughgoing overhaul of school culture where people's behavior changes, school structure changes, the school changes, and student learning improves. Learning communities are not an appendage to traditional school culture; they replace the traditional school culture (DuFour & Fullan, 2013).

A MAJOR OBSTRUCTION TO DEVELOPING LEARNING COMMUNITIES

Around the same time that the concept of learning communities started to become popular, there was also another emerging concept, school accountability. Many in society, in business, and in government were expressing growing disappointment in the outcomes of schooling. These critics pointed to low test scores, high dropout rates, unskilled graduates, low graduation rates, and the fact that students in many foreign countries scored better than American students on international standardized tests. These critics understandably wanted schools to be more accountable for positive results.

One of the outcomes of this disappointment in schools has been that important people in Washington, D.C. and in state capitals have lost faith in teachers and local school leaders. These policymakers came to the conclusion that if local school leaders and teachers could not run effective schools on their own, it would be necessary to impose on them mandates and standards that would require positive results. Moreover, these mandates and standards would be enforced by a variety of funding and disciplinary devices.

With a genuine desire to get better results from our schools, central policymakers have attempted to take greater control. To assert this control, states have for a long time been requiring students to pass standardized tests in order to graduate. Authorities were no longer willing to trust teacher evaluation of students as legitimate indicators of learning. All teachers know, of course, that these standardized tests have taken a very imposing presence in our schools.

More recently, the federal government in the No Child Left Behind legislation has required schools to show annual improvement in student learning as reflected in standardized test scores. This legislation includes some harsh consequences for schools and their leaders if the standardized test results indicate little or no improvement in learning for individual students and for a school overall.

Most recently, the Race to the Top legislation has required that teacher evaluations be at least partly based on the standardized test scores for students in a particular teacher's class. If students in a particular class show little or no improvement in learning, that teacher could face difficult consequences or be dismissed.

As this effort of central authorities to take control of our schools has unfolded, the important decision making for schools has moved away from local school and community stakeholders to central policymakers outside of the school. The decisions are often made by people who have little experience in classroom teaching and no knowledge of particular schools, their populations, or their unique conditions.

In the face of all of this, teachers find themselves increasingly marginalized as thinkers and decision makers. They see that in spite of their stakeholder status, their influence within their schools is diminished with each new mandate. Teachers watch with frustration as forces outside of schools dictate standards, goals, curricula, lesson design, and even what teachers should say in delivering a lesson. Teachers are even faced with talk in policy circles of "teacher proofing" instruction.

This marginalization of teachers as engaged stakeholders in their schools is borne out by timely research. A recent Gallup poll indicated that "among all occupations tracked in their survey, teachers were the least likely to say that their opinions counted at work" (Busteed, 2014). Moreover, in that same survey teachers were last "in agreeing . . . that their supervisors create an open and trusting environment" (Busteed, 2014). This is remarkably dark data considering that it comes more than twenty years after the advent of learning communities was roundly and loudly embraced by many leaders in education, including those in Washington, D.C.

Add to this condition teachers' deep unhappiness with a variety of new evaluation systems that they see as unfair, the plummeting career satisfaction data reported by the MetLife Foundation (2012), and the recent observations of the famed classroom teacher Rafe Esquith, who complained in *Educational Leadership* of teachers being "the scapegoat for factors beyond their control . . . and the unfair, often ridiculous expectations being placed on teachers" (Esquith, 2014, 20).

So moved by the adversity that contemporary teachers face, Nancie Atwell, winner of the coveted Global Teacher Prize, explained in *Education Week* that "public school teachers are so constrained right now by the Common Core Standards and the tests that are developed to monitor what teachers are doing with them" that "if you're a creative, smart young person, I don't think this is the time to go into teaching unless an independent school would suit you" (Moeny, 2015).

In light of all of this, is there any mystery to the old but persistent statistic: nearly 50 percent of all new teachers leave the profession within their first five years of teaching (Ingersoll, 2012)? This evidence points to an obvious conclusion. The promise of the learning community model has never been realized.

THE NATION'S REPORT CARD

This book is about teaching. Teaching is about the facilitation of student learning achievement. Thus, there is yet another reason to redirect aspiring teachers: the traditional school structures that have marginalized teachers as thinkers and decision makers have also done little to improve student learning for decades.

To find out how all of the accountability efforts have turned out, the reader may refer to what is commonly regarded as the nation's report card, the National Assessment of Educational Progress (NAEP). This assessment instrument is the outcome of congressional legislation and is administered by the Department of Education. The well-regarded test is given annually to find out what progress students in fourth, eighth, or twelfth grade are making.

In reporting the following information to the reader, it should be clarified that NAEP is considered by the U.S. government to be the nation's report card. It is not cherry-picked negative data to suit this book's argument. As it turns out, in spite of many years of accountability testing and billions of dollars spent, the report card is not so good. A report on the long-term trends in student reading and math achievement based on NAEP scores reads "average reading and math scores in 2012 for 17-year-olds were not significantly different from scores in the first assessment year" (IES, 2012).

Note that the first assessment year was 1971. So over the course of more than forty years, there has been no notable improvement in student performance in math and reading. Add to this that the number of students who achieve a score of proficient in the various other tested areas such as writing, history, or biology remains consistently below 50 percent, some much lower.

THERE MUST BE A DIFFERENT FUTURE FOR FUTURE TEACHERS

The premise of this book, then, is that as we prepare aspiring teachers for a future of teaching, we must prepare them for a different future. It cannot be a future where teachers are the pawns of central authorities in state capitals and Washington, D.C. Instead, it must be a future that strikes a clear contrast with conditions today. The table below, informed by self-determination theory and research, clarifies that contrast.

When you look at the previous table, would you really consider directing young, aspiring teachers into the same conditions our teachers face today? Would you have them learn to expect to be compliant implementers of others' decisions? Or, is it better to establish the expectation in them that their future in teaching will be an outcome of their collaboration as thinkers, creators, and decision makers working together to improve themselves as teachers and to improve their schools?

Think of it this way: Teaching is your profession. You are its steward. Clearly, for lack of asserting ourselves, the teaching profession has gone adrift and now finds itself in troubled waters. One way to correct our course is to point the way for the next generation of teachers to a professionalism that is healthy and self-directed. Aspiring teachers need to be pointed in the direction of all of the professional, personal, and student learning benefits inherent in the learning community model.

A Career of Frustration Today	A Satisfying Career in the Future
Lack of Self-Determination You lack a sense of control over your work. For the most part, the nature and design of student work, its implementation, and its evaluation is dictated by legacy practices of federal, state, or local officials or publishers with whom you have little contact and who do not ask your opinion.	**Self-Determination** You have a sense of purpose and feel control over your work. You make important choices and play a key role in the design, execution, and evaluation of your work.
Sortive Evaluation You feel little power over your own evaluation. You believe there are factors included that should not be there and other important factors left out. You see the process as a way of sorting teachers and not very helpful in supporting your improvement as a professional.	**Supportive Evaluation** You inform how you are evaluated. You have helped design the evaluation process. You play a critical role in how the process is applied. You believe the others involved in your evaluation care about you and are supporting your growth as a professional.
Teacher Technician You see yourself as a worker/technician tasked with implementing standards, goals, curricula, lesson design, and even scripts dictating what you should say in delivering lessons to students. You are never asked to reflect on or give judgment about what is being taught, how it is taught, or the overall assumptions and practices of your school.	**Teacher Professional** You are a member/stakeholder. You feel like a respected member of a professional team. You helped the team create a vision for optimal functioning, and you work collectively with it to learn and to take action to apply that learning. As part of this, you are often called upon to bring your judgment and imagination to important decision making.
Lack of Community The school you work in is large. There are many hundreds, maybe more than a thousand, students and over a hundred staff. Many people don't know or care about each other. The friendships that form are part of cliques that are unrelated to the school's goals and culture. There is often animosity between groups. Student and adult behavior often shows disconnection and disregard for others. There is a lot of negative gossiping and complaining. Students' achievement is usually the outcome of compliance or competition, not high engagement.	**Caring Community** The school you work in is a deliberately designed small community with the stated purpose of creating a culture of caring where both adults and students are committed to a high level of kindness and respect for all members. Members feel connected and cared about. They believe that such a caring community is the foundation for human engagement in life and learning. Caring and engagement are seen as the basis for high expectations and high achievement.

Technical Learning

Your professional learning is focused on the implementation of standards created by others and preparing students for success on an array of standardized proficiency assessments and year-end standardized tests created by others. Neither you nor other teachers are asked to reflect on the value of these standardized tools nor many of the other assumptions and practices of your school. If you disagree with their use, you are regarded with suspicion. A lot of research, including research suggesting the ill effects of standardized testing, is overlooked. You experience a high level of frustration as you realize that your thoughtfulness and its role in your professional growth is being ignored.

Professional Learning

You are aware that your school community is heavily invested in your professional learning. There is ongoing reflection on the effectiveness of a broad array of learning and schooling strategies for both students and teachers. Professional learning is embedded in your everyday routines. Research is happening everywhere. There is a collective eagerness to consider imaginative and entrepreneurial ideas for change and improvement. You enjoy your continuous growth in competence within this culture as you take on new challenges and ever greater responsibilities.

Introduction

Students Have Access to Two Perspectives

As this book looks to help the teacher of aspiring teachers guide students in thinking about what it means to be a teacher, it will seize on a unique situation. The first part of that situation is that students can easily access and reflect on what it is like to be a student. For example, students know how they experience, think, and feel about the various situations they are exposed to in their classes and other school activities, and they know what some teachers do that really make them want to learn and what others do that make them not care and want to escape.

If students have never taken time to reflect on "how I experience school," this book will help teachers with that, too. An important idea in this book is that teachers and students should spend a lot of time reflecting on what they do in school. Teachers should always be asking, Is what I'm doing in my classes really helping students, or should I try something new? Students should be asking, Is what I am doing in school really helping me, or do I need a new approach? Such reflection and discussing it with others stands to lead to improving what students and teachers do at school.

The second part of your students' unique situation is that they want to be teachers so they are also thinking about the teacher perspective, too. They may wonder why teachers do the things they do, say the things they say, or even why school is set up in the way that it is. And even if they are not sure about the perspectives of teachers, they are in a place where they can easily ask you or other teachers to tell them what their perspectives are so they can think about them and discuss them with their teachers. An important aspect of this book is to present students with situations that they should discuss with their teachers. Sharing perspectives is key.

An important premise of this book is that this situation in which students have easy access to student and teacher perspectives puts them in the best possible position to think about becoming a teacher. In fact, it is arguable that secondary school, not college, is the best place to start preparing to be a teacher, even if students are not sure yet that they want to be teachers. What they stand to learn in secondary school could divert them from a mistaken choice or propel them into the career of their dreams. And there is more.

There is not only ready access to teachers to discuss their experience as teachers but also these additional benefits to starting teacher preparation in secondary school:

- It is a good place for students to learn that school is a place where teachers not only design learning for students but also design learning for themselves, too.
- In learning how to design learning, there is more room for students in secondary school to influence what happens in their school by imagining, starting, and building their school's unique teacher preparation program.
- The interaction of students and teachers in creating such a program will be conducive to everyone rethinking the nature of teacher preparation.
- The interaction of students and teachers in creating a teacher preparation program will be conducive to rethinking the nature of school itself.
- This kind of involvement will encourage "design thinking" among students who will be designing their own learning and the learning of others later.
- Secondary school students stand to bring "fresh eyes," "fresh voices," and less compliance to the concept of what it means to be a teacher.
- Secondary schools have more flexibility than colleges to allow more student enterprise and experimentation in discovering the nature of teaching and what it means to be a teacher.

It is also important to understand that when students leave secondary school, they will likely lose touch with the student perspective as they start to think of themselves more and more as traditional teachers. They will certainly lose touch with their easy access to teachers because they will no longer be situated in a K–12 school system. So it is a much superior situation to get students thinking about what it means to be a teacher while they are still secondary school students and have good access to two perspectives.

Thinking about how these two perspectives relate to each other will also prepare students to face one of the most important concepts in teaching and schooling, community learning. Students are likely to find the concept very appealing as they are listened to by teachers and helped to see that community learning is about people who work together and who make a deliberate effort to care about each other, share perspectives, learn together, and do that learning in order to improve how they work and learn together. It is a cycle that leads to continuous improvement of any organization or school.

It is via this process of having aspiring teachers examine how students experience school and how teachers experience school that the best possible teacher preparation will happen. It is with this examination as a basis that aspiring teachers and their teachers can begin a process of sharing perspectives and talking about the realities of teaching and schooling. By developing this dialogue and working together, they will thereby see themselves creating the foundation for optimum teacher and student learning. That optimum foundation is the formation of a learning community.

Finally, secondary school is also a formative period where the compelling value of the learning community model has a chance to override the traditional notion of a teacher's work. Appreciating the value of the learning community model stands to improve students' choices for higher education as they consider very traditional, status quo programs or programs that promote the learning community model.

SHARING PERSPECTIVES AND THE LEARNING COMMUNITY MODEL: A DIFFERENT FUTURE FOR FUTURE TEACHERS

Learning community experts Richard and Rebecca DuFour, Robert Eaker, and Thomas Many have expressed it well in their book *Learning by Doing: A Handbook for Professional Learning Communities at Work.* They explain that "the most promising strategy for helping all students learn at high levels is to develop a staff's capacity to function as a professional learning community" (DuFour et al., 2006, 1–2).

As this book unfolds, it will clarify the full meaning and promise of the learning community model. It will demonstrate to the reader, the teacher of future teachers, why the future of teaching will be much brighter if the learning community model is established as our profession's goal and the right destiny for all our future teachers.

In doing so, the book will develop a variety of areas for consideration by teachers of future teachers and their students. These Benchmarks in the Evolution of Teaching will all be natural extensions of the learning community model as they all have to do with coming together to share perspectives, inquiring into the conditions of learning, forming goals for improvement, and taking collective action for continuous school improvement.

SCHOOL: CARING, SHARING PERSPECTIVES, LEARNING, AND WORKING TOGETHER

The concept of community learning might be understood even better if you and your students consider these three questions, questions that they will want to answer as they envision their careers as teachers:

1. Do I think people who work together in a school should care about each other and take care of each other?
2. Do I think it is important for me, a student, to consider how my teachers experience school and the challenges of teaching students?
3. Do I think teachers should try to understand how I and all students experience school and the challenge of learning from teachers?

Your students would probably say yes in answer to all of these questions. It seems only reasonable that people who work together should try to understand each other and give each other time to express their views and even to influence how things go. But such a reasonable answer leads to facing a difficult issue: research shows that listening to students' perspectives is not a big part of school life in most schools (Holcomb, 2007; Mitra, 2008). Wonder why not?

If your students become teachers, will they make a point of listening to students? Why would they do it? Why would it be important for a teacher or a school leader to hear from students about how they see what happens at school? After all, what do students know that would be important for the adults to know? Can your students think of anything?

Ask your students to consider how often at your school students are asked about how they experience school and what opinions they have formed about it. If their opinions are listened to, do they see that the adults have made significant changes based on student input? Most likely, they don't see this. Research indicates that it rarely happens (Mitra, 2008, 9). Do your students think that students who are not listened to really feel cared about?

BRINGING STUDENTS INTO THE LEARNING COMMUNITY

The idea of teachers inviting students into the learning community may strike you as new and unusual. It may even seem radical, and it may put you on edge. If any of this is true, it is quite understandable. Most schools do not invite students to share their perspectives on how they experience school or how the school might be improved. It is just not what we do in traditional schools. In light of this reality, the reader's patience is requested in understanding the rightness of this approach.

The fact is that the idea is not a new one. There are some schools that invite students to work with teachers on how to improve instruction and how to improve the entire school experience. Many scholars have written reports on the benefits of listening to students and how it benefits students, teachers, and the entire school to make students real members of the learning community (Byrnes, 2005; Cook-Sather, 2000, 2002, 2006; Cushman, 2010; Fielding, 2003; Holcomb, 2007; Joselowsky, 2007; Mitra, 2004, 2008; Rudduck, 2002; Senge et al., 2000).

LEARNING IN COMMUNITY IS BETTER

There are probably many reasons why learning in a community is good for everyone, but in this book three will be emphasized. One, learning and growing happen best in the context of caring relationships. As a teacher, you probably remember some teachers who took an interest in you, which inspired you to get involved, do your best, and learn more. Many teachers report such experiences in their personal journeys.

In those moments you probably noticed, too, that you started to feel more caring about that teacher. Maybe you felt some empathy when you saw your teacher dealing with a tough situation. You felt your relationship.

There is even a sense in which one might say that learning is about relationships. Think about it. It is through relationship with our parents, people at our houses of worship, at Scouts, at other community functions, and, especially, at school that spur young people to achieve and become the kind of people they dream of becoming. Behind so many of the things we learn in life, there is almost always a caring relationship.

There is a second reason. When people who care about each other deliberately share perspectives in order to learn together to improve what they do, it usually leads to the idea of making some changes. If students and teachers took time now and then to share perspectives and reflect on what they do, they might also come up with the idea of trying new ways to think about learning and to improve learning experiences. Certainly, it makes sense to do that.

Students and teachers might even discover that when they make such changes that it makes them happier. They might feel more comfortable with the new experiences they have provided themselves. They might observe an increase in learning. They might even begin to find their work more fun and exciting.

As students and teachers working together experience the benefits of making changes, they might begin to feel that continuous change and improvement should be one of the primary purposes of their work. It makes sense for people in a school to want to continuously improve learning. With this kind of open reflection, they might begin to push the evolution of learning into previously unexplored areas.

A third reason is that doing things as part of a community is great preparation for teaching and living. When your students eventually become teachers, they will work in a school community and a greater living community. This will require strong skills in working with others. Researcher, student advocate, and author of *Students Are Stakeholders, Too!* Edie L. Holcomb (2007) put it well when asking,

> Why are schools putting things into mission statements like "becoming contributing members of society" and "productive citizens in a global economy" and "lifelong learners" but not granting full participation in the immediate society around them—their school community? (Holcomb, 2007, 7)

When you think about it, this idea of community learning sounds wonderful, but there is one big problem that you need to consider as a teacher of future teachers. As Edie Holcomb has suggested, most schools generally do not do this. You probably already know that. Students and teachers generally don't work together to share perspectives and think about how to improve learning at school. In fact, to some people the idea may seem unrealistic and ridiculous.

What may seem even more ridiculous is the idea of having a school where people really care about each other. Let's face it. Schools can be really lonely places for a lot of kids and socially treacherous for everybody (Olson, 2009). Teachers are often too busy and stressed with their own responsibilities to give students the attention they need or want. Having to teach and get students to learn all that is required these days for standardized tests often conflicts with developing a caring atmosphere at school (Hebert & Durham, 2008).

Add to that the reality of student cliques, name calling, vicious gossip, hard competition, and outright bullying and school can be a very rough place, even in nice communities. The very idea of students caring for each other and their teachers would probably seem like a joke to many. It is easy to understand that the idea of a school where students and teachers function as a caring community must seem very unrealistic. Still, this book is about teachers leading the way in remaking our schools into caring communities, and that includes making students part of the learning community.

A CAREER-CHANGING EXPERIENCE

The reader deserves an explanation about why the author is so enthusiastic about listening to student voices and developing caring communities. It is not just about being nice to students.

One day, late in his career, the realization came: students have great insights into teaching and learning at school. Sadly, the realization came as a big surprise. The situation was this: A secondary school had a partnership with a local university that prepared teachers. As part of the partnership, aspiring teachers at the university would come to the author's secondary school for various activities and just to observe and experience the day-to-day operations of the school.

On one particular day, the secondary school held a fishbowl activity for the university students. It went like this: About a dozen secondary school students were assembled into a circle, and the author sat among them as the facilitator. Then the aspiring teachers from the university were assembled around the secondary school students. Thus, there was a kind of fishbowl where the university students could watch and listen to the secondary school students, although the university students would not participate in their discussion.

During the discussion session, the high school students were given these directions: Today you are going to be asked to tell what it is that teachers do that make you want to learn. There will be no complaining and no naming of teachers. We want to hear from you on one topic: all the things that your teachers do that make you want to learn.

After giving these directions, it became quite obvious that the secondary school students seemed very pleased, even honored, to be part of this activity. They really wanted to share their observations on this topic, and all were very thoughtful as they reported various experiences from teacher smiles, exciting projects, acts of personal caring, and many more. What the author was most impressed with was how grateful students seemed to be to be included in this activity. For them it was great to know that teachers cared enough to ask for their insights.

After the session was over, there were refreshments and time for everyone to talk to each other about the value of the experience. As the author went around and thanked the secondary school students for their participation and greeted university students, he secretly felt ashamed. This experience had been earth shaking. In that one-hour session, he learned things he had never thought about before. And it all came from listening to students, something he could have easily done before.

He was also deeply impressed with how inspired students were to have been included and listened to. It made such a big difference to them. Each was eager to participate. Everyone sat up straight and thought carefully about all of their remarks. They often struggled to explain complex things they believed were important for adults to understand. But as he considered it all, he felt his face turn red with shame.

Why shame? It was because this important learning had come late in his career. He questioned himself, "Why didn't I learn the importance of listening to students earlier?" This shame and disappointment was heightened when he spoke with the university students and they also confirmed that they had learned a great deal from listening to the students, much of which they said "was not in our textbooks."

Hopefully, this will clarify for readers why this book makes the student perspective so important. It's not just a way of being nice to students. Listening to student voices is a real part of how we can make schools better. Since then, the author has made a break with business as usual and done extensive research listening to student voices, which has led to the writing of this and other books.

From the perspective of both students and of teachers, the reader is asked to consider what it feels like to know that you are being listened to, to know that your opinions count. Does it make you eager to learn, to try harder, to want to contribute even more?

But also, consider the opposite. What does it mean to know that your opinions don't matter? Does it make you eager to learn, to try harder, or does it make you want to give up, to not care, and to just want to get out of the situation? Of course, you know the answer to these questions.

LEARNING IS ABOUT RELATIONSHIPS AND PARTICIPATION

Think of it this way: Everybody wants to be included. Everybody wants to be listened to. Everybody wants to participate. It's frustrating to sit on the bench and watch other people make the important decisions and big plays. It makes you feel unimportant. Everybody wants to be part of the action.

And when people are included, listened to, and encouraged to participate, they become more inclined to think and reflect. They become more energetic and more disposed to ask good questions and come up with good ideas for improvement. In fact, one could say that learning is about participation (Brown & Adler, 2008). That will be a recurring theme in this book. And if that is true, shouldn't teaching be more about getting everyone involved, about everyone participating, about learning and working as a community?

Even though you might agree that all of this is true, you probably also recognize that most schools don't spend a lot of time trying to hear the student perspective. It's not business as usual; it's just not what schools do. Some recent research even found that when adults did try to find out what students were thinking and feeling, the students were so skeptical that many said that they didn't trust that the adults would make any changes with the information they got (Yazzie-Mintz, 2009).

What should be appealing to your students about the programs of action described in this book is that it guides students in trying to realize real community in a school, to see it as an integral part of a teacher's work.

Secondary school students are, of course, very sensitive about inclusion issues, and they are likely to find their leadership in building community a very compelling task.

In providing students opportunities for deep thinking and active, hands-on learning, this book will develop as follows.

"Part 1: Being a Teacher in the Future," takes a strategic look at what it means to be a teacher and how the evolution of teaching stands to enhance that meaning.

"Chapter 1, Developing a Vision: Helping Students Imagine Themselves in a School of the Future," tries to give the reader an idea about where the evolution of teaching might go in the future. It provides a glimpse of the future by outlining some of the characteristics of a twenty-first-century school and how it comes from the full participation of all members sharing perspectives and trying to improve learning. It will place special focus on having your students examine what in their own personal journeys has pointed them to the profession of teaching.

Chapter 2, "Your Students' Leadership: It Begins with a New Mindset," has to do with your mindset as a student in a traditional school where student voices are not heard. That mindset needs to change so you begin to believe in your capacity to have an impact on your school. This chapter explains how the voices of students helped inspired this book and calls on future teachers to assert leadership by hearing all voices and contributing to the overall humanization of schools.

Chapter 3, "Your Students' Career: Staying with the Past or Leading into the Future," discusses the concepts of bureaucracy and standardization as important concepts in twentieth-century schooling. It further describes the inability of adults to let go of these concepts as drivers of educational policy and practice. It details the effect of standardized testing and the effects of twentieth-century thinking on students. In all, the chapter presents a choice between a new way of looking at education based on the learning community concept or staying with a one-size-fits-all, standardized approach to schooling and learning.

Part II, "Benchmarks in the Evolution of Teaching," is devoted to clarifying what aspiring teachers need to look for as indicators of progress as young educators attempt to lead the evolution of teaching.

Chapter 4, "Teachers Learn and Teach Twenty-First-Century Skills," presents the concept of twenty-first-century skills and shows how it supports the idea of learning communities as a great way to learn the skills necessary in the twenty-first century. It further shows why it is important to apply the Common Core State Standards to teacher learning as a way of supporting their twenty-first-century skills.

Chapter 5, "Teachers Recognize Quality Levels in Learning," discusses in teenage terms what research has suggested for decades. Student learning achieves different quality levels depending on the goal that motivates learning. Too often those goals lead to cheap, low-level learning just "to look good," and the idea of authentic learning is neglected.

Chapter 6, "Teachers Invite Students to Share Their Voices," is a chapter devoted to understanding how listening to students can actually lead to better teaching and better schools. It reviews recent research about the benefits of listening to students.

Chapter 7, "Teachers Facilitate Greater Individualization of Study," focuses on how listening to students will clarify for adults that although all students want to learn, they do not all want to learn the same things at the same time in the same way. In the future, teachers will focus more on the individualization of student studies.

Chapter 8, "Teachers Investigate Students' Learning Engagement," discusses the idea of actually enjoying learning and the concept of school engagement. It clarifies for students that schools should be assessing student engagement as they work through the curriculum, but also that most schools don't do this. The chapter guides students through engagement assessment exercises and asks prospective teachers to evaluate the importance of understanding students' engagement.

Chapter 9, "Teachers Elicit Intrinsic Motivation" and 'Knowing Myself as a Learner,'" illuminates a different path to authentic learning through understanding one's own characteristics as a learner and one's intrinsic motivation. It also provides an exercise for understanding one's self as a learner. It asks students to consider why their teachers rarely express interest in students' unique characteristics as learners and why they should in the future.

Chapter 10, "Teachers Stop the Game of School," introduces the concept of the game of school, a cultural phenomenon in which students only pretend to learn. It will help students understand the effect of bureaucracy and standardization, how it leaves students and adults feeling powerless, and leads to the game of school. It further clarifies how a different school culture could eliminate the game of school.

Part III, "Leading the Evolution of Teaching and Learning," focuses on getting a better picture of how schools of the future might be different as a result of your students' leadership.

Chapter 11, "The Story of Jane," provides an example of how a student and a teacher working together were able to create an individual learning path that helped Jane take ownership of her learning and take an active interest in helping others do the same.

Chapter 12, "Let's Imagine a Twenty-First-Century Secondary School," guides students through an exercise that helps them begin to envision twenty-first-century teaching and a twenty-first-century secondary school experience. It clarifies how such an education breaks with twentieth-century thinking while also encouraging deeper learning in traditional subject areas and providing better preparation for college or a twenty-first-century workplace.

"The Action Manual—Your Leadership Now Leads to Your Leadership Later" brings students back to the idea of the importance of sharing perspectives and working as a community in creating twenty-first-century schools. In doing this, it asserts the importance of students learning from active, firsthand experience. It asks students to assess their own motivation to influence how teaching and secondary schools will change. It invites students to enlist communal support from students and teachers so they may take action to create a full program of teacher preparation in secondary school.

TEXTBOX I.1 TEACHERS LEARNING

A Prompt List
For Thinking about and Creating Secondary Programs for
Aspiring Teachers

Review these recommendations. Then design your own program.

1. This program would be presented to students as one of elite status. Entry into the program would require at least two qualifications: 1) a record of commitment to doing well in school, and 2) a record of commitment to good citizenship as stewards and helpers of youth.
2. The students invited into the course must be committed to completing a program of rigor and significant achievement.
3. The suggested name for this program is **Teachers Leading**.
4. Participating schools would commit to installing a Teachers Leading Program as a major subject to be completed by participating in both a future teachers club and the completion of coursework.
5. The course component would involve a student taking two major 5 credit courses about teaching. These courses would be treated as major subjects and would involve the rigor that would clarify that an individual student is, in fact, of the high quality that the teaching profession needs.
6. These courses would be taught or guided by teachers or administrators of widely recognized pedagogical distinction.

7. At the core of this course would be orientation to the professional learning community model where students would work in collaborative teams to assess various conditions in their school and work collaboratively to understand them and improve them. The concept of **continuous school improvement** would be a motto of the program.
8. As one objective of the Program would be the recruitment of highly qualified candidates, students in the Program would be treated with a high level of deference and the Program (including the courses) would provide many of the active experiences which students prize such as class trips, conferences, guest speakers, cultural events, project presentations, panel discussions, inter-school visitations, action research projects, contributing to research publications, actual teaching in classrooms, apprenticing with veteran teachers and more. *The course would not be textbook-teacher talk centered. It would be student action centered.*

I

Being a Teacher in the Future

Chapter One

Developing a Vision

Helping Students Imagine Themselves in a School of the Future

When students begin a project like the one outlined in this book, it is always good for them to have some idea about the end result, to know where their efforts will take them. What's more, when any person or group undertakes to create change, they need to have a vision of the final result—what they want to accomplish. Facilitating students developing such a vision is the purpose of this chapter. The importance of students developing a vision of change is doubly important in this case because it is potentially about their full careers of thirty or forty years.

Developing such a vision of a new kind of school that students will really believe in is not such an easy task. Many organizational and educational researchers have documented ad nauseam the inability of people to break from their notion of a traditional school (Senge et al., 2000; Kelly et al., 2009; Waters, 2014). Because the structure, practices, and cultures of traditional schools are so firmly set in our minds, it is often difficult for most people to imagine how a school would be different. When challenged with imagining such a school both young people and adults find themselves asking, "Well, how could a school be different?"

In this regard, let's consider the end result of students and teachers sharing perspectives while learning and working together. Let's imagine such a school. Following are points that attempt to describe such a school of the future.

- As a learning community, students and teachers are continuously working together discussing what learning means and how to do it better.

- Teachers are empowered as leaders of school operations and in the development of learning strategies.
- The learning community has well-defined goals for continuously improving care and services for students.
- Each student is known by teachers in a deep way, and teachers try to build on students' talents and intrinsic motivation.
- All members of the learning community take responsibility for making learning fun and exciting.
- What students learn is relevant to their lives now and in the future.
- Each student has an individualized program of study.
- Student voices and opinions play an important role in school operations.
- Each student gets the individual attention she or he needs and wants.
- Students are encouraged to be self-directed in their learning.
- Students routinely invent their study topics and even invent courses.
- Students feel ownership over their learning lives.
- Sometimes students work alone, sometimes in groups.
- Students are important partners in helping teachers improve learning and instruction.
- Student assessment is informed by students and focuses on artifacts that demonstrate mastery and learning, which are kept in an electronic portfolio. There is much less focus on grades.
- Most classes are active/project based: way less sitting and listening to teachers talk.
- Time structures are reinvented to include earning credits 24/7, year round.
- Classes extend out into the community, often involving community partners for community improvement.
- There is less competition, low drama, and high emotional and spiritual support.
- Student learning is deeper, more authentic, and more personal than in a traditional school, and students will be better prepared for college, work, and a full life of learning.

This list is presented to the teacher of aspiring teachers and their students because a primary purpose of this book is to help everyone imagine new kinds of schools where teachers (and students) play new, more influential roles as members of a learning community. They will be schools where teacher and student opinions do count.

Perhaps now you can think of some description points that you would like to add to the list above. That would be great. The list above is not a final list. Hopefully, as you and others do a lot more reflecting about schools and how they might change, many more points might be added to this list, or a completely new list could be created. The point is to get people thinking more, sharing perspectives, and working together to create better schools.

CONCLUSION

Given the conditions discussed so far, this book looks to influence young aspiring teachers to greater participation and leadership in their schools. That includes now while they are secondary school students and later when they go to college, and much later when they become practicing teachers. This book hopes to support you as you create in them the expectation that they will become respected professionals whose opinions will be asked for and who will be included in leading and making important decisions for their school. Being a teacher means thinking, participating, and leading, and future teachers will have important roles to play.

If getting your students to think of themselves as decision makers and leaders who people will listen to sounds like the kind of professionalism you want for them, then you have caught the spirit of this book. You may even be thinking about some changes you would like to discuss with others that would change conditions for teachers today. Hopefully in the future it will be part of a teacher's work to design schools and to continuously redesign them as conditions change and new visions emerge.

DISCUSSION QUESTIONS BEGIN THE LEARNING COMMUNITY PROCESS

Discussion Questions and Leadership Activities like the ones that follow will come at the end of each chapter. They are included in this way not by convention but by design. Providing questions and then activities follows the idea that in a learning community, teacher learning will involve sharing perspectives, discovering and gathering new information, clarifying goals, and then taking action to make changes to improve schooling based on what was learned.

DISCUSSION QUESTIONS

1. The learning community model implies students and teachers sharing perspectives, learning together, and taking collective action to improve a school. Why do you think such collaboration is or is not a good idea?
2. How do you respond to the idea that the next generation of teachers will need to create new kinds of schools around the learning community model?
3. Have you started to envision anything else that might be added to the descriptive list of a new kind of school presented in this chapter?

LEADERSHIP ACTIVITIES

1. Break your class up into small groups. In those groups, come up with a list of five ways schools should be different in the future.
2. Conduct a survey of teachers. Ask every teacher to tell you one way that they would like teaching to be different for the next generation. (Give them overnight to think about it. Provide the question one day, and pick up the answer the next.) When you look at all of the answers, how does that affect your thinking about how teaching should change in the future?

Chapter Two

Your Students' Leadership

It Begins with a New Mindset

The program of teacher preparation in secondary schools presented in this book challenges students to think of their future work as teachers in ways different from the present. This redirection of student thinking is proposed because veteran teachers shouldn't want the next generation of teachers to face the same conditions teachers are facing today. We want future teachers to take control of their profession and direct it to a better place.

Presenting this challenge to students will likely be somewhat confusing to them. They will certainly want to know why change is necessary and if they have the capacity to lead change. This chapter is about helping future teachers start to believe that they can meet the challenge. And they can best be prepared to meet that challenge by starting work now in asserting a new mindset while still in secondary school.

As this book unfolds, it will present readers with a variety of benchmarks by which a new generation of teachers might measure progress in their efforts to change and improve schools. These benchmarks will signal improved conditions for both teacher development and student learning. The book will end with an Action Manual. That's right. It is about how secondary school students can take action and make a difference in their schools right now.

It is very important to remember that none of the information or advice on taking action will be meaningful if students don't believe that they are capable of influencing change. So, again, this chapter is about getting students to believe in themselves and their capacity to influence their schools, influence the teaching profession, and influence change.

INSTILLING A NEW MINDSET BEGINS WITH LISTENING TO STUDENTS

Getting students to believe that they can be change agents is going to begin with you, their teacher, listening carefully and taking their perspective seriously. You should make it clear that you do not discount their views as just students complaining. It must be conveyed to them that many of their concerns and complaints as students have validity and may very well warrant efforts to change the school.

The process of listening to students should be part of an ongoing class discussion that may be prompted in this way:

1. Ask students to examine themselves and how they experience school in general. What do they feel good about? What do they feel bad about? Ask them how they could improve as students. Ask them how the school could improve in helping them to succeed.
2. Ask students to reflect on their classroom experiences at school. They should ask themselves, What is helping me learn? What is not helping me learn? What is valuable? What is a waste of time? How could my teachers help improve my learning? How can I get more engaged? How will my work as a teacher be different in the future?
3. Prompt them to also discuss their concerns with all of their teachers. Encourage them to meet with as many teachers as possible to have discussions about the best conditions for learning. Encourage them to pose good questions to teachers and school leaders about why things are the way they are and how they might be improved.

When students have been listened to in earnest and prompted to engage in a sharing of perspectives with teachers and other students, they should have developed a basis for believing that their perspectives are important and the school improvements they ultimately decide to pursue will be valid.

STUDENT VOICES INSPIRED THIS BOOK

The author is a career secondary school teacher who, for many years, worked with college and secondary school students who wanted to become teachers. This involved working with secondary school students in classes for aspiring teachers. It also involved helping to create a professional development school in partnership with a university to help novice teachers move their learning out of college classrooms and into actual schools to learn from experienced teachers in a real school setting.

These experiences led to another important turning point in his own learning. It came while doing research in a secondary school with students who were in a class called Tomorrow's Teachers. During many discussions with these students, it was discovered that they believed something that was not true (Waters, 2012).

Students believed that secondary school could only be the way they knew it and experienced it. There were no other choices. It could only be the traditional secondary school that they, their parents, and their grandparents knew. It was then that it became clear that this book had to be written.

The students who were part of the research project didn't really know much about recent and important changes that had taken place in learning and education. All they knew was what was happening in their secondary school which, again, was like most secondary schools in the United States. These students had never heard of any secondary school being different from theirs.

Even you, the reader, when you stop to think about it, may also find it hard to imagine a different kind of secondary school. What would it look like? How would it be different? This book is going to help you answer those questions.

Meanwhile, in talking about learning and life at school, the student participants in the research explained that they would actually prefer a school that allowed them more time to focus on learning in subjects in which they were personally interested, as opposed to all of the requirements that were forced on them. In other words, students would have liked to have programs of learning that were more individualized and customized to their own learning needs and interests.

When this author heard the students saying these things, he responded enthusiastically by telling them that such individualized programs were a good idea and a possibility even though they were not available at their school right at that time. Having said this, he was amazed when the students didn't believe him and responded by saying they didn't think such individualized programs were "realistic."

In disbelief, students responded, "How could a secondary school give all students an individualized program of courses that they were actually interested in? It doesn't seem possible." In the face of this disbelief, two things became apparent. One, the students had no confidence in their own ideas about school. Two, they didn't believe anyone would want to hear their ideas anyway.

Considering these students' outlook, it was very disappointing that secondary schools were influencing students to just accept secondary school as it was—not to examine their experiences, not to share perspectives with others, and not to raise questions about how to improve. This experience made it clear that schools needed to change and that this book had to be written in order to get secondary school students, especially aspiring teachers, to believe in their ideas and their capacity to improve their schools.

A NEW MINDSET IS NEEDED

As some of the problems we currently see in our schools have been described in this book, some of your students may have found themselves asking this question: Who am I to be criticizing my school? The question is understandable. Your students are only secondary school students. Their school was created and is being run by many well-educated adults who, on top of that, are really fine people. So who are your students to be raising tough questions and making criticisms?

While these concerns are understandable, teachers should reassure students that asking tough questions, making criticisms, and suggesting new ways of doing things should not be considered impolite or disrespectful to the adults around school. While students should always be respectful of others regardless of their age, schools are places for thinking. No one should be offended by aspiring teachers and their teachers sharing their thoughts and suggestions for a better school.

A key point here is that students and teachers raising questions about what goes on at school should not seem unusual or stressful. It should be the norm. Students and teachers should work as a community that constantly reflects on what it does, and plans change on the basis of its reflection and learning.

In a sense, then, this book is asking aspiring teachers to take on a new mindset and to help establish a new norm in our schools. It will be a norm of sharing perspectives, learning together, and making changes for continuous improvement.

CONCLUSION

The point of this chapter has been to clarify that as you read and apply this book, mindsets should start to change. Slowly, thoughtfully, your students should start to think of themselves as thinkers and leaders who want to be heard and who expect to influence their school. Developing this personal mindset will play a critical role in becoming the kind of teachers we need in the twenty-first century. Secondary school is a great place to develop that mindset through practice. As you lead students in this transition, you might have them discuss the following illustrations.

Perspectives on Time

I Look to the Past

"My ideas come from the past.
I feel comfortable with what I'm used to.
My mind is made up.
I like tradition.
I often say, "I don't know…Wait…But…Be realistic"
I like the way we have always done it
I like to remember.
I like the tried and true.
I don't like criticizing what took hard work and years to establish.
I feel comfortable with familiar routines.
Routines get things done. They are automatic.
I worry about what is coming next.
I think those change-people are unrealistic.
I see things falling apart and trouble coming for our schools.
I like discipline and compliance.
I'm worried about losing my position.
So what if the world has changed."

I Look to the Future

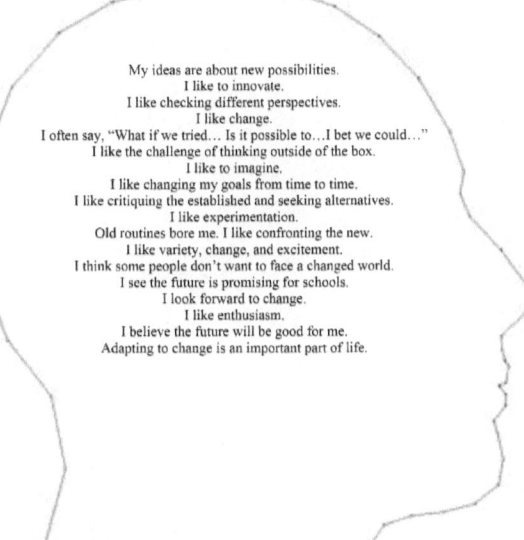

My ideas are about new possibilities.
I like to innovate.
I like checking different perspectives.
I like change.
I often say, "What if we tried… Is it possible to…I bet we could…"
I like the challenge of thinking outside of the box.
I like to imagine.
I like changing my goals from time to time.
I like critiquing the established and seeking alternatives.
I like experimentation.
Old routines bore me. I like confronting the new.
I like variety, change, and excitement.
I think some people don't want to face a changed world.
I see the future is promising for schools.
I look forward to change.
I like enthusiasm.
I believe the future will be good for me.
Adapting to change is an important part of life.

Figure 2.1. Perspectives on Time I Look to the Past / I Look to the Future

DISCUSSION QUESTIONS

1. After having considered the previous illustrations, describe your mindset. Do you think that students should be listened to more? Do you think students should be able to influence their school to change?
2. What kind of leadership do you foresee will be necessary to convince school leaders that listening to students is a good idea? Will that same leadership also help teachers achieve greater influence in their schools?

LEADERSHIP ACTIVITIES

1. Get your students to speak out. In one of their classes, don't complain, but ask to have a discussion on a topic in which they think students need to be heard. Then, if they were successful in starting a discussion, ask them how that success felt.
2. Have students start keeping a notebook of practices and procedures in your school that don't work very well; that is, they don't improve learning. Have them start imagining new practices and procedures that should be given a try. Have them share these ideas in class.

Chapter Three

Your Students' Careers

Staying with the Past or Leading into the Future

This book has a point of view. It expresses the belief that along with teachers, *students have important opinions about teaching, schooling, and learning*. This is especially true for students who aspire to be teachers. This chapter is about the long-term implications of students and teachers listening to each other and sharing perspectives.

This idea that students and teachers should exchange perspectives on learning, teaching, and instruction is not exclusive to this book. University research has shown that secondary school students have valuable things to say about teaching and learning (Byrnes, 2005; Cook-Sather, 2000, 2002, 2006; Cushman, 2010; Fielding, 2003, 2004; Holcomb, 2007; Joselowsky, 2007; Mitra, 2004, 2008; Rudduck, 2002, Rudduck & Flutter, 2004; Senge et al., 2000).

Unfortunately, another line of research has also shown that students don't think that their opinions are considered important by the people who run their schools (Yazzie-Mintz, 2009). Thus, this chapter is devoted to clarifying for students that as they look to create a different future for the teaching profession, inviting greater voice and influence for students is the right thing to do. This outlook should be bolstered by the previous citation of the many psychologists and educational researchers who agree that it would be good for students to be part of a school's learning community and to be able to influence what and how they learn. And again, that is extra important for students who want to become teachers.

To the aspiring teachers in your class, this idea of asserting themselves and working together with teachers to change and improve schools must seem like a no-brainer. So why don't schools just make some changes and start doing it?

There is a simple answer to this question. The people who lead our schools can't envision change. Because of something in their outlook, most people in schools want schools to stay the way they have always known them. You might say they have a model of a school in their heads that they know from the past and they cannot get away from that model. It's a kind of comfort zone.

As a teacher of aspiring teachers and an educational leader, that might even include you. Yes, *you*. And it probably includes the students you are teaching. Without some influence from you and this book, the students you work with now are likely destined to become traditional teachers in traditional schools and suffer the same powerlessness and marginalization that currently plagues the teaching profession. This is why aspiring teachers now must become accustomed to being assertive and exerting influence in their schools. It must become their way of being.

SCHOOL BLINDNESS

The vast majority of people in the field of education, adults and students, develop a unique mental condition, a kind of ailment. Think of it as a type of blindness. It might be called "school blindness." Inside that blindness, a person can see, but she or he can only see what has been seen before. They can never see something new. People with this blindness come to believe that only the past is real. New things seem unreal. When a new vision is presented, those with this blindness will automatically say, "That is unrealistic." In other words, that new vision cannot be real because it is not part of the world that has been seen before.

Please consider whether you or your students have school blindness. Right now when your students look forward to their careers as teachers, they probably see themselves standing in front of a classroom teaching a lesson in a traditional school, probably like the one they attend right now. In that school, all of the things that you know make up a traditional school are happening in the normal way they have always happened. The traditional school has become their reality.

This book is intended to help you help your students step out of that reality and to help them help others to step out of that reality. It will encourage you to create a new reality, a better reality. In fact, that new reality will not only be better, it will keep getting better all of the time because continuous improvement will be a part of the new reality. Change will never seem "unrealistic." In the new reality, change will be the norm because things keep getting better and better.

WHAT CAN THEY SEE?

To further examine the extent of you and your students' school blindness, how would you and they honestly answer the following questions: Can you and they envision a school where:

- Students and teachers are really working together as a community?
- Teachers know all students in a deep way?
- All members of the learning community take responsibility for making learning fun and exciting?
- What students learn is relevant to their lives now and in the future?
- Each student has an individualized program of study?
- Student voices and opinions play an important role in school operations?
- Each student gets the individual attention she or he needs and wants?
- Students are encouraged to be self-directed in their learning?
- Students routinely invent their study topics and even invent courses?
- Students feel ownership over their learning lives?
- Sometimes students work alone, sometimes in groups?
- Students are important partners in helping teachers improve learning/instruction?
- Most classes are active/project based: way less sitting and listening to teachers talk?
- Classes extend out into the community, often involving community partners for community improvement?
- There is less competition, low drama, and high emotional and spiritual support?
- Student learning is deeper, more authentic, and more personal than in a traditional school, and students will be better prepared for college, work, and a full life of learning?

When you are responding to these questions, how many times did you or your students find themselves saying, "That is unrealistic"? Many of these new visions are hard to accept because they are not part of our past experience. Neither teachers nor the students should feel stupid if anyone found some or most of these ideas unrealistic. At the same time, all should remember that school blindness might be the cause. This is already known because schools like those described above already exist.

THE LEGACY OF NOT LEARNING TOGETHER, NOT WORKING TOGETHER

The fact is that everybody gets comfortable with the way things are. And when change comes, there is always a lot of resistance. People complain and get upset. This happens even when the change is clearly for the better. Still, the fact remains that when people get comfortable with doing things one way, they don't like to change.

How does the author know this about schools? Besides having worked in many schools and read many studies about schools' resistance to change, there is one gigantic piece of evidence: our schools do not change. Our schools today, except for having become larger, have not changed. They are about the same in design as schools one hundred years ago.

Think about it for a minute. Schools are almost exactly the same as they were when your teachers were in school. Schools are pretty much the same as when *their* teachers were in school and *their* teachers, too. The current design for schools was, in fact, modeled after Industrial Age factories with a big focus on standardization so everybody did the same things at the same time.

The design of our nation's public schools is older than black-and-white TV. In fact, it is older than TV itself. The current design for schools is older than the telephone, the airplane, electricity in houses, and even the Model T Ford.

Think about how much the world has changed in just the last ten years, and then think about secondary schools not changing for the last one hundred years. Why? The answer is that the people who run schools just like them being the way they have always been. It feels comfortable (Kelly, McCain, & Jukes, 2009).

Here are some of the things that cause adults to resist change. They like thinking that school is where you learn all the important things in life. And they love thinking that all important learning comes from classroom instruction. They like having a certain number of classes (five, six, seven, eight) every day. They like having school for ten months every year. They like the idea that school starts in the morning and ends in the afternoon. They like the idea that all of the "learning" happens in the same building, the school.

School leaders like the idea of giving students grades (A, B, C, D, F), of giving students awards (journalism award, athletic award, scientific project award), and of giving students a rank (top ten and so on). They believe all of this will make students work harder. They like the idea that all of the classes are lined up along the hallways so they are easy to check on. They like the idea that what you are supposed to learn is neatly separated into subjects like math, history, English, biology, and so on.

The leaders also like the idea that teachers teach a certain number of classes each day and that everything students should learn is outlined in the curriculum so teachers know what they are supposed to teach from day to day. They like the idea of having a lot of required classes with just a few electives.

They like the idea of secondary school lasting exactly four years (but it could be two years for some students and five years for others). They like the idea of using textbooks so everything the students have to learn is neatly put together in one place. They like the idea that by teaching those classes every day, teachers will earn their salary for the year.

Everyone likes that after thirty years or more teachers and administrators can retire and get a nice pension. In general, the people who run schools feel comfortable with the whole system. It's orderly, controlled, and predictable. In fact, when you ask the adults about how schools might change, you can see they feel a little stumped. They ask, "Really, how else could a school be?"

As a teacher of aspiring teachers, doesn't it strike you as strange that during more than a hundred-year period, the adults never engaged in the kind of reflection that would lead them to find a reason to change a single one of the traditional practices mentioned above, not one of them? There is a reason. *The leaders can't envision change!*

How about you? At this point in reading this book, are you convinced that schools need to change, that the work of teachers needs to change? How will that affect how you influence your students to lead?

SCHOOLS PROCLAIMED THEY WERE CHANGING, BUT THEY DIDN'T

Consider this: More than thirty years ago, in 1983, a famous report on American schools was published. The report was called *A Nation at Risk: The Imperative for Educational Reform: A Report to the Nation and the Secretary of Education, United States Department of Education* (United States: National Commission on Excellence in Education, 1983). The report suggested that students were not learning enough in schools and that schools needed to change for many reasons.

Since that book was published there has been a vigorous discussion among adults in government, in colleges and universities, and in primary and secondary schools among teachers and school leaders about how to change our schools. More than thirty years later, the outcome of all of this discussion is no change. The curriculum and physical structure of our schools remain pretty much the way they were a century ago. The adults with all of their talk about "reform" were unable to change schools. Why? The reason is simple: adults don't really want to change!

While this accusation may seem harsh, remember that all this time the adults were in charge of schools. During that time, schools did not change. Who else could be responsible? Also, note that the author looks back at his career with great regret because he did not influence change, although, like others, he did talk about it a lot.

This situation should make you happy that you chose to become a teacher of aspiring teachers. Why? Because it begs for new leadership. It is an opportunity for you to step up and guide your students to a new place. Ask yourself this: Do I want students to go off to teach in schools that never change? Or do I want them to teach in schools that evolve, that accept change as part of life and change when learning suggests a better way of doing things?

There is an important thing to remember, however. The schools we have now were designed in the Industrial Age (late 1800s) and were not designed for the sharing of perspectives with the purpose of changing from one year to the next. Their design did not include the idea of students and teachers thinking, reflecting, and learning together for the purposes of coming up with ideas for change and improvement.

STUDENTS HAVE BEEN TOTALLY LEFT OUT

When American schools were first designed back in the 1800s, the idea of adults seeking students' ideas and opinions for change would have been laughable. However, in the last thirty years or so, there has been more openness to the idea of listening to students, but few schools have actually done it. That will be discussed in an upcoming chapter. Still, in the last thirty years, while adults have had vigorous discussion about school reform, one group, students, has almost always been left out, and the other group, teachers, was often included but more for show than real involvement and decision making.

Leaving students and teachers out was a huge mistake. It is an even a bigger mistake because of the effects on students who aspire to become teachers. As students, they get used to being left out, so when they become teachers they have become used to it. They become used to being told what to do. Following orders becomes second nature. Their leadership is frustrated.

UNDER PRESSURE, SCHOOLS PRETENDED TO CHANGE

Earlier it was explained to the reader that central authorities in state capitals and Washington, D.C., were trying to take greater control of our schools. As they did this, they also put pressure on schools to show that they were changing in ways that would improve learning.

As a result, the people who lead schools have become sensitive about the topic of change. They know that people are talking about how schools are not doing a very good job and how they have pretty much stayed the same for over a hundred years. So these school leaders are always starting up these little projects that they call "school reform." Like pretend learning communities, there has been extensive pretend school reform. Meanwhile, schools have pretty much stayed the same.

School leaders start these projects to show that they are changing. The teachers and school leaders get the parents involved, have community meetings, and put articles in the newspapers and journals. Educators have been doing this since back in the 1950s.

But here is the problem: after schools go through these "school reform projects," they always end up with the same school they had in the first place. No real change. (Supowitz & Weinbaum, 2008; Kelly et al., 2009)

SCHOOL BLINDNESS LEADS TO MORE OF THE SAME CHANGE

Because of school blindness, a favorite approach of adults to change is what might be called "more of the same change." This is what educators have been doing for the last thirty years or so since the publication of *A Nation at Risk*.

This is how it worked: When important government reports, legislation, or funding suggested that schools needed to change, the adults came up with an approach to change that didn't change things. The adults didn't consider that maybe they needed to change some of their ideas about schooling—about when it happened, where it happened, or how it happened. It didn't occur to them that schools might have different goals, different structures, or different cultures.

Instead, school leaders intensified what they were already doing. For them, changing meant doing an even better job at what was already not working. So, we got:

- more and harder standardized tests
- more instructional focus on standardized testing
- more and harder required subjects
- more teacher-centered-teacher-talk instruction
- more Advanced Placement and Baccalaureate programs
- more central control
- more rules
- more penalties
- more surveillance

- more pressure
- more supervision
- more and bigger textbooks
- more homework

Because of school blindness, youth didn't get new kinds of schools. They got more of the same change.

The reader has already seen a description of a new kind of school. A new kind of school is possible. They do, in fact, already exist. Although there are relatively few of them, there are a number of examples to consider. What is most inspiring is that these examples come from innovative public schools led by forward-thinking public school teachers who created real change. An example will follow each benchmark chapter in Part II of this book.

CONCLUSION

Chapter 3 has clarified a choice for future teachers and their teachers: stay with the past or lead into the future. That future will be about schools where the voices of students and teachers share perspectives and work as a community for the continuous improvement of a school.

QUESTIONS FOR DISCUSSION

1. Having read this chapter, explain why you do or do not want a future where students and teachers have greater influence in their schools.
2. Who do you think should do the important thinking and decision making for schools?
    a. all the stakeholders in a school: students, teachers, school and community leaders
    b. just the school administrators
    c. people outside the school, like the board of education, county administrators, state administrators, or people in Washington, D.C.
3. Do you think the idea of students having more influence is a positive idea for the future? Is it realistic?

LEADERSHIP ACTIVITIES

1. Students should request to attend a session when teachers in their school are working as a learning community.

2. As a function of their learning community, students should set up a special forum to discuss this book and the outlook for the teaching profession with teachers and school leaders.

II

Benchmarks in the Evolution of Teaching

Chapter Four

Teachers Learn and Teach Twenty-First-Century Skills

Part I of this book dealt with considering what it means to be a teacher. This is important because what teachers think it means to be a teacher will influence how they choose to behave and the kinds of schools they will create in the future. There was special emphasis on teachers sharing perspectives with each other and with students as the driving force behind improving student and teacher learning.

Chapter 3 discussed the reluctance of many educators to change our schools and move away from the traditional school model, a model where students and teachers have little voice in the operation of schools.

What follows in Part II turns away from the past and looks to the future. To help measure progress in that future, benchmarks are presented that will help your students measure their progress as their teaching careers unfold. These benchmarks will indicate real movement away from the traditional school model and toward a model that emphasizes the importance of people sharing perspectives and working as a learning community.

TWENTY-FIRST-CENTURY SKILLS

The first of these benchmarks is the inclusion of twenty-first-century skills in both student and teacher learning. In response to the many complaints with which our schools were faced in the 1980s, 1990s, and early 2000s, several groups sought to advance the discussion about how to fix our schools by putting forth their own ideas about what students should learn in schools. Three of the most prominent and powerful groups were the Partnership for

21st Century Skills, the National Governors Association, and the Council of Chief State School Officers.

According to these groups, the primary concern was preparing students to meet the demands of the twenty-first-century workplace. In their view, our schools needed to educate students as more self-directed, intentional learners. Students needed to be self-starters with the ability to apply the customary content knowledge they learn in schools to solving workplace problems, dealing with unpredictable situations, and fostering innovation.

These concerned groups along with many educators came to believe that this fundamental change away from the focus on memorizing information to the application of knowledge would make students more effective citizens, learners, and workers in the twenty-first century (CCSSO, 2009; Partnership, 2007; NGA, 2005; Senge et al., 2000).

In support of this goal, the Partnership for 21st Century Skills advanced a specific list of skills that it argued were necessary for effective participation in a twenty-first-century workplace. This list has received the support of academic, governmental, and civic organizations (CCSSO, 2009; NGA, 2005; Partnership, 2005) and is presented in their document *21st-Century Skills, Education & Competitiveness: A Resource and Policy Guide* (2007).

The twenty-first-century skills cited were:

- Flexibility and adaptability
- Initiative and self-direction
- Social and cross-cultural skills
- Productivity and accountability
- Leadership and responsibility
- Creativity and innovation skills
- Critical-thinking and problem-solving skills
- Communication and collaboration skills (13)

As a teacher of aspiring teachers, you are asked how any student would learn such skills of personal effectiveness. There is an obvious answer: by employing these skills throughout their schooling.

LEARNING COMMUNITY SKILLS ARE TWENTY-FIRST-CENTURY SKILLS

The most important point here is that the skills cited above are, in fact, the very skills needed for and developed in a learning community. They include working with others, thinking critically, solving problems, being productive, and being accountable while asserting creativity to innovate and continuously improve the work of the learning community.

What was important about the Partnership's list is that it highlighted the reciprocal relationship between core content knowledge (the things we remember and understand) and the ability to apply that knowledge via the cited personal effectiveness skills. In other words, twenty-first-century employers are interested in *what students can do* with what they know.

The list recognizes the idea that knowledge and its application are part of the same whole. Each informs the other. In order to function optimally in the twenty-first century, youth entering higher education or the workplace must have not only core content knowledge but also the ability to apply that knowledge in diverse and unpredictable situations (Brown & Adler, 2008; Scott, 2010).

Research indicates that this focus on application skills in education accurately reflects the expectations students will face when entering the world of work (Chew, 2009; Jaros & Crick, 2006; Scott, 2010). In that regard, Black (1997) has observed, "Workers think, give opinions, are listened to and have real decision-making power because [as exclaimed by Deming] *no one else has their direct access to information*" (cited author's emphasis), and "a much more self-directed and individualized end product is expected" (11–12) of schools.

SUPPORT TWENTY-FIRST-CENTURY SKILLS FOR TEACHERS

One can see from the previous quotations from educators that what the twenty-first century demands most of it workers is that they be critical thinkers who can solve problems and innovate. Unfortunately, embedded in this effort to help students learn twenty-first-century skills is an ugly contradiction. The teachers who are expected to teach twenty-first-century skills to students will not be asked to learn or use them.

Stated another way, the professional learning provided teachers in their teacher preparation programs and in the schools where they work do not emphasize the acquisition and application of twenty-first-century skills.

The absence of this emphasis becomes apparent if we revisit the Gallup survey that found that of all the occupations tracked in their survey, teachers were the least likely to say that their opinions counted at work (Busteed, 2014). If teachers do not feel that their opinions count at work, what kind of learning could be going on? What kind of thinking? What kind of collaboration? What kind of perspective sharing? What kind of critical and creative brain storming for continuous improvement of their school?

APPLY THE COMMON CORE TO TEACHER LEARNING

As a teacher of aspiring teachers, you need to understand why this condition exists and how it came about. Earlier it was explained that in order to gain greater control of schools and to ensure learning in them, most states in the United States began to institute big standardized tests to check that students were learning and to prevent their graduation if they were not. This eventually led to the idea that states should clarify exactly what it is that students should learn by creating a set of learning standards.

While some states did start to develop their own standards, someone came up with the idea that there should be one set of standards for the entire United States. This idea caught on.

The National Governors Association and the Council of Chief State School Officers endorsed this project hoping to prompt schools to high levels of achievement. This ultimately led to the creation of the Common Core State Standards. Like the twenty-first-century skills, they highlight application skills such as critical thinking, adaptive learning, problem solving, and creativity, along with core content knowledge.

By last count, the vast majority of states decided that they would implement the Common Core State Standards. While the CCSS is a very helpful document, it is deeply flawed on two counts: (1) for failing to recognize and account for the influence of school design on student learning (in other words, learning is not just about classroom instruction but also the design of a school), and (2) the negative effect forced implementation of these standards would have on teacher learning.

As the teacher of aspiring teachers, please take a minute to reflect on how the following scenario affected teachers recently and how it will affect teachers in the future: By state legislation, teachers were told that they would begin using the Common Core State Standards. Teachers in local schools were not involved in creating the standards they thought would be appropriate to their unique schools. They never were asked to evaluate the CCSS for application in their local schools. They were never asked to consider the CCSS as a starting point for creating a set of standards appropriate to their local community. Instead, they were just told they were going to begin implementing the Common Core State Standards.

The point is that when you just tell teachers to implement standards, you take away the opportunity for them to think. You take away the opportunity to evaluate those standards for local application. You take away the opportunity to act creatively and to innovate. In effect, teachers were denied the use of the very skills that they were expected to teach. They were not asked to do the very things that build twenty-first-century skills in them.

Unfortunately, this issue of denying teachers learning opportunities does not end with the standards. With the standards imposed on schools, then the goals and objectives of teaching are also influenced. We see now that textbook publishers are already proclaiming that their products are aligned with the Common Core and thus indicate the appropriate goals and objectives of teaching. Not allowing teachers the opportunity to designate the appropriate goals and objectives of student learning is another learning opportunity lost for teachers.

With these goals and objectives determined by others, the actual design of lessons also become increasingly predetermined by the alignment of standards, goals, and objectives. Thus, textbook publishers often provide teachers guides with directions on how to conduct lessons, including what to say, in order to keep student work aligned with the Common Core State Standards.

The effect of all of this is that teachers are being denied the chance to assert creativity in creating lessons and in designing the learning experiences of students. Instead, the work of the teacher becomes standardized, mechanical, and technical as they follow canned directions to implement the designs of people they do not know and who have never set foot in their schools. Clearly, teachers are *not* being prompted to learn or apply twenty-first-century skills.

What constrains the thinking and creativity of teachers even more is the standardized tests that come ever more frequently in our schools. Teachers are under tremendous pressure to make sure students do well on these tests. And remember, more and more, these tests are aligned with the Common Core and all of the aligned goals, objectives, and curricular content, little or none of which was determined by teachers. In effect, the role of the teacher is more about following directions than acting as thinkers.

Again, with this arrangement, teachers are not being asked to collaborate, to evaluate, to think critically, to act creatively, to solve problems, or to design better ways for their schools to function. In each case with respect to standards, goals, objectives, lesson design, and school design, someone else does the thinking. It is the very opposite of twenty-first-century skills, and it leaves little mystery as to why teachers were the least likely to say that their opinions counted at work (Busteed, 2014).

This dilemma is brought to the attention of aspiring teachers and their teachers because clarifying the skills most important to the twenty-first century is a good idea. Students should learn these skills. There is an important reason for this. When students enter the workplace, the most common scenario will be that they will work as part of a team. In that team they will be expected to think critically and creatively, to collaborate and communicate effectively, all with the purpose of solving problems and creating innovation.

What better place to learn these skills than in a learning community where they will use them on a regular basis. Both teachers and students will better acquire these skills when schools become learning communities.

CONCLUSION

Part II of this book shifts the reader's focus away from the problems of the past and focuses attention on contemporary solutions in learning. One of the primary developments in learning in recent years has been the designation of twenty-first-century skills, a set of personal effectiveness skills that emphasize an individual's ability to apply content knowledge in the workplace and higher education. Add to this the advent of the Common Core State Standards, which also focuses on critical and creative thinking in collaboration with others.

What is significant about both of these developments is that they support the importance of making schools into learning communities where people develop the habits of working together, solving problems, and thinking creatively for continuous improvement of the school. The idea of twenty-first-century skills supports the importance of students and teachers sharing perspectives and working together in learning communities.

DISCUSSION QUESTIONS

1. Explain what it means that twenty-first-century employers are more interested in *what employees can do* than what they know?
2. How do you understand the difference between book learning and personal effectiveness?

LEADERSHIP ACTIVITY

In learning community groups, design a lesson that focuses less on remembering and more on personal effectiveness.

TEXTBOX 4.1. PUBLIC SCHOOL TEACHERS ARE LEADING THE WAY LEARNING TWENTY-FIRST-CENTURY SKILLS

In their book *21st Century Skills: Rethinking How Students Learn*, editors James Bellanca and Ron Brandt include an article by Richard DuFour and Rebecca DuFour titled "The Role of Professional Learning Communities in Advancing 21st Century Skills." They highlight the need for teachers to practice twenty-first-century skills while they facilitate students learning them. DuFour and DuFour explain, "The Partnership [for 21st Century Skills] called for schools to be organized into 'professional learning communities for teachers that model the kinds of classroom learning that best promotes 21st century skills for students'" (DuFour & DuFour citing Partnership, 2007, 77).

DuFour and DuFour provide the example of Adlai Stevenson High School in Lincolnshire, Illinois, where "a teacher's contribution to his or her team is a significant factor in his or her evaluation because the collaborative team is regarded as vital to the effectiveness of the school. The time for collaboration that is built into the school calendar each week provides teachers with the continuous ongoing professional development credits required for their ongoing certification. The school offers its own graduate courses, taught by its own staff, on topics that represent priorities for the district, and those who complete courses receive credit on the salary schedule. The success stories of collaborative teams are told at every faculty meeting, and a team reports on its work at every meeting of the board of education. Everything the school does—professional development, scheduling, rewards, and recognition—is designed to support the message that helping all students learn at high levels requires a collaborative and collective effort" (DuFour & DuFour in Bellanca & Brandt, 2010, 89).

Chapter Five

Teachers Recognize Quality Levels in Learning

Part II of this book focuses on benchmarks to watch for in changing the roles of teachers and pushing the evolution of learning and instruction. Chapter 5 focuses, in particular, on a learning issue few recognize: Learning has quality levels. In other words, it is possible to learn something at a very shallow, meaningless level, and it is possible to learn the same material on a deep, meaningful level.

A big problem for schools now is that students can be successful in school while learning mostly on a shallow, meaningless level. As a teacher, you probably know about this because you see students learn material or complete projects just to get them done and get the grade they want. Contrary to the very notion of twenty-first-century skills, students ask for precise directions so they can make sure they give teachers what they want. You may, in fact, have done this when in school yourself. This author did. It is shallow, strategic learning that is quickly forgotten.

With that in mind, the obvious question becomes, How can schools be changed so student learning is of a deep and meaningful quality? The fact is that students can be guided in a different direction. You may have even noticed that occasionally one of your students will undertake a learning project with a lot of personal enthusiasm and ownership. This student has a different approach to learning. She enjoys it.

The idea that learning has quality levels is actually an idea based on the observation, experimentation, and conclusions of many researchers (Ames & Archer, 1988; Bain, 2012; Blackwell et al., 2007; Dweck & Leggett, 1988; Entwistle, 1977; Fransson, 1977; Gibbs & Taylor, 1982; Grant & Dweck, 2003; Hong et al., 1999; Martin et al., 2005; Marton & Saljo, 1976; Mueller & Dweck, 1988; Rossum & Schenk, 1984).

But without knowing about the details of all of this research, you can probably see in your own school experiences that some students just learn what they need to learn to get the grades that they want while others actually get involved in what they are learning and make a personal investment in it.

So the idea that learning has quality levels is not exactly a huge discovery, but it does help with this question: What can schools do to get away from the shallow, memory-based learning that is commonplace in our traditional schools now and get students involved in learning where they get deeply into it and make a personal investment?

Guiding your aspiring teachers to consider these quality levels will likely surprise them to some extent. Most people, including teachers, take it for granted that school is about strategic learning to please the teacher and get the grades you need. Asking your students now how schools might be changed to get students to make a greater personal investment in their learning may pose an unexpected challenge.

Along with this question in mind, you and your students should consider a few other questions about the goals of learning.

- What is the purpose of learning?
- What is the purpose of knowledge?
- How should knowledge be used?
- What is the purpose of going to school?

How anyone answers these questions should give them a good lead in thinking about quality levels in learning.

As you and your students consider that most students in schools work just for grades and a minority of students work hard because they enjoy it, what does it make you think? Ask each of your students to explain what is true for them and why. Ask them to explain what influences students to become different in this way. Can they imagine what caused one to just learn for grades and the other to learn for a personal purpose?

These questions get at the issue of why the next generation of teachers might want to change schools and what teachers do in them. Moving our schools into the twenty-first century is about providing students with a better quality of learning. It will be learning that students undertake because they have a personal motivation, and they are willing to make a personal investment in it.

When you reflect on these questions with your students, ask them to consider the following. Like most people, secondary school students like to get the most for their money. Like most people, they like to get high-quality stuff. But if their education has been gotten in schools that have a student culture of "getting grades to look good," like most schools, then they are *not* getting a high-quality education. They are getting the cheap, low-end, dollar-store stuff.

In a "look good" kind of school, students don't get together with teachers and school leaders and reflect on the quality of learning. They just keep focused on getting the grades they need regardless of the quality of learning. And remember, even the kids who are going to Harvard get low-quality learning when all they do is focus on grades and achievement.

What's worse is that these same kids may continue to get that low-quality learning at Harvard because they have learned in their schools to keep focused on grades, not learning. So the problem is what students are taught about the goal of learning. What should the goal of learning be? Is it all about looking better than others, or is it about something else, something about personal identity, fulfillment, curiosity, exploration, growth, expressing a passion, experiencing joy?

It is the students who have somehow learned to love learning who are getting a high-quality product. These students often go to different kinds of schools. The culture of the school is one of ongoing reflection with teachers and other students about how students experience and benefit from their studies. Students and teachers are always openly talking about how learning can be gamed or not gamed and made personal and authentic.

In such a school, students and teachers seek out learning experiences to which students will commit and work hard because they love the experience, not because they want to get a high grade so they can get into a fancy college. Teachers are committed to creating learning experiences that get students fully engaged and give them the kind of all-in experience they will need in the twenty-first-century workplace.

It is noteworthy that research has shown that students often seek out their own learning projects for personal reasons. These projects are often very complicated, time consuming, and educational (Childress, 2000; Cushman, 2010; Damon, 2008; Waters, 2014). Typically, students get no rewards for undertaking these projects except the enjoyment of the project itself.

The grades for the student who has learned to enjoy learning are probably not as good as a grade grubber's grades. Such a student probably doesn't do everything in his life so he will look good to his teachers or college admissions officers, and she probably doesn't feel constantly pressured to overachieve. But as such students explain, their learning provides them with many positive experiences, chief of which is a sense that the learning has personal meaning and provides a sense of ownership over it.

Such students understand why they are learning the things they have chosen to learn and how they fit into their developing sense of purpose and what they want to do in life. What they choose to do in life will be done because it is meaningful and they enjoy doing it, not because they want to look good to others. By the way, many of the students who learn to learn authentically will ultimately far outachieve the greediest of grade grubbers.

WHICH KIND OF STUDENT SHOULD SCHOOLS ENCOURAGE? IN WHICH KIND OF SCHOOL DO YOU WANT TO BE A TEACHER?

TEXTBOX 5.1. HOW WILL A TWENTY-FIRST-CENTURY SECONDARY SCHOOL BE DIFFERENT?

A twenty-first-century secondary school will offer learning that is individualized, personalized, and informed by the learner. Students will be offered ownership of their learning, and they will continuously make choices about what they learn. All students will have their own unique learning path. Students will focus on learning how to learn what they want to learn. Their learning will be infused with continuous reflection on life's purpose, the nature of learning itself, and what makes learning personally meaningful. In this context, learning will be customized to the needs, strengths, weaknesses, intrinsic motives, and goals of the learner.

Twenty-first-century secondary schools will take the approach of individualization, personalization, and customization of learning because society now has the capacity to offer it to youth and because such an approach is supported by research as a better way of schooling.

Ten Indicators of Twenty-First-Century Teaching and Learning

Look around your school. Do you see any of these indicators?

1. Teachers take time to understand an individual student's uniqueness as a learner, and they encourage the student to reflect on that uniqueness and her goals in learning.
2. Teachers and students work together to create individualized learning plans that students may pursue for credit year round.
3. The school employs a variety of data-driven strategies for individualization of learning, educational counseling, and career counseling such as Wireless Generation, Knewton, Learning Catalytics, Match.com, Naviance, ConnectEDU, eAdvisor, or Degree Compass. (You can ask your administrators if the school uses these tools.)

4. Each student moves through school at his or her own pace, and students are able to skip taking basic courses by demonstrating they already have the knowledge and skills via a test or project.
5. Students are provided special courses or learning modules outside of the regular curriculum that may help them with unique strengths, interests, needs, or weaknesses. For example, students are referred to StraighterLine, General Assembly, Skillshare, MOOCs, or netTrekker to find supportive learning resources or to YouTube for both remedial and supplemental learning or to Khan Academy for help with math. Teachers may also access high-quality and specialized instructional plans for students at Teachers Pay Teachers, which is a marketplace where teachers sell and share some of their finest instructional planning.
6. Students' technology skills are continuously improved in step with the rapid evolution of personal technology devices and learning online, both at home and in school, as a regular part of the schooling routine. Moreover, as part of helping students stay on technology's edge, students are involved in games to learn technology.
7. Schools are reaching out to the wider communities to expand resources that allow them to offer educational programs as provided by other agencies such as the fire department, police department, or local hospital or by local experts in a variety of fields.
8. Students are able to earn credits from other reliable agencies of certification that support youth development such as scouting organizations, boys and girls clubs, libraries, YMCAs and YWCAs, summer institutes, travel institutes, and others.
9. Credits may be earned in a wide variety of knowledge and skill specialties commensurate with students' individual learning profiles and achievement goals. These merit badge–style credits may come from the students' secondary school or another facility as students are encouraged to create their own projects or courses as individuals, as groups, or in coordination with teachers in their schools or from the community.
10. Students are helped by adaptive learning technologies that assist students in the mastery of information and skills via interaction with a computer program that adjusts to student competency levels while instructing. Examples of such commercial products are WebLearn, eSpindle Learning, Knowre, PrepMe, or Smart Sparrow. In addition to instructing, some of these programs contribute or collect data on students' behavior, choices, and performance around school, in classrooms, and online to give students

> feedback on where their passions lie, what their strengths are, where they need help, and which higher education options will likely be best suited for the students' advancement.

All of this information should lead students to several questions. What kind of teacher do I want to be? Do I think that some of the suggested changes in school designs and teacher practices are good ideas? Would I like to know more about schools where these new designs and practices are working?

Regardless of what you and your students are thinking, the important thing is that everyone is thinking, and everyone knows that there are choices. If your students want to be teachers, they don't have to be traditional teachers. In fact, the main idea of this book is that you and your students should be thinking about how teaching and schooling need to change to make them better.

CONCLUSION

Part II of this book is about benchmarks that indicate movement away from the traditional notion of teaching and learning and toward a new model. This chapter has focused on one particular benchmark, becoming aware of quality levels in learning. We know now that our traditional schools allow students to succeed by relying on memorization and doing things to look good instead of truly getting involved in and personally invested in learning.

QUESTIONS FOR DISCUSSION

1. How can you tell if your school has a culture that emphasizes learning to look good or learning for personal growth and enjoyment?
2. Can you identify and describe instances when you learn just "to look good"?
3. Can you recall a time when you learned something because you actually wanted to learn it and you enjoyed the experience?

LEADERSHIP ACTIVITIES

1. Design and take an informal poll to determine how frequently students in your school learn because they actually enjoy it.
2. Have a discussion about learning experiences that you enjoyed for their own sake. Do you see a pattern emerge about what makes learning enjoyable?

3. Design a learning experience for your learning community that you believe would facilitate learning that is enjoyed for its own sake.

TEXTBOX 5.2. PUBLIC SCHOOL TEACHERS ARE LEADING THE WAY ACKNOWLEDGING QUALITY LEVELS IN LEARNING

High Tech High School is formally known as the Gary and Jerri-Ann Jacobs High Tech High Charter School of San Diego, California. It is one of a number of charter schools operated under the broader organization of High Tech High Charter Schools. High Tech High has a deliberate focus on deeper, reflective learning and students taking ownership of their learning. As captured in the student testimony below, the school rejects the memory-based learning of traditional schools.

High Tech High is a project-based learning school. Textbooks are instruments used by traditional schools to get students to memorize the material, then take a test on it, but it doesn't prepare students for the whole other side of education. Here, the goal as a school is to teach concepts in ways in which we can figure how we got to our resolutions, and to be able to structure our education by ourselves. Students have a big role in the High Tech High school, and greatly impact the curriculum for the classes as well. Whether in Student-Led Conferences with parents and teachers, or in POLs (Presentation of Learning), students always have the floor when it comes to talking about their process in their education. High Tech High not only aims to hear from the students in their process but also to hear them reflecting on what their different work in the school has brought out in them, and what they have gained from it. High Tech High is truly an amazing school. (www.greatschools.org/california/san-diego/11837-High-Tech-High/)

In his book *World Class Learners: Educating Creative and Entrepreneurial Students*, Yong Zhao explained that High Tech High follows four design principles distilled from the findings of the New Urban High School Project (The Big Picture Company, 1998): personalization, adult world connection, common intellectual mission, and teacher as designer. He also cited a study from the Buck Institute for Education (2009) that concluded that such programs were responsible for "building deep content understanding" as opposed to the strategic book learning that happens in most traditional schools (Zhao, 2012, 194).

Chapter Six

Teachers Invite Students to Share Their Voices

This chapter is about how listening to students can point the way to better schools. It will report recent research that shows how the student perspective provides important insights about school and how schools and teaching might be improved.

Yes, listening to students in this way is a big departure from the traditions of the past, but there are good reasons for it. This chapter will, in fact, demonstrate that inviting students to express their opinions is not just about being friendly to students. It is about better learning in schools. Hearing the voices of students on how they experience school should be regarded as an important benchmark in our progress toward creating learning communities and improving teaching.

In her book *Student Voice in School Reform: Building Youth-Adult Partnerships That Strengthen Schools and Empower Youth*, student voice scholar Dana L. Mitra (2008) makes the case that

> youth-adult partnerships such as student voice initiatives have been shown to have powerful benefits for the young people involved. Research has found young people who participate in youth-adult partnerships tend to have an increase in confidence and leadership and attachment to social institutions and to foster a range of competencies. (11)

Right now you probably teach in a secondary school where students' opinions about important school issues are never asked for. For example, probably no one has ever asked students about what the rules should be, what the penalties for broken rules should be, what subjects should be taught, or at what times they should have to go to school.

In fact, it may seem crazy that this book would even suggest that adults should encourage students to have opinions and choices about any of these. In traditional schools, others usually set all of the rules, people who the students and teacher probably don't know. The subjects students study are "required" by unknown local, state, and federal authorities, and what times students should attend school were probably decided by unknown school leaders many years ago.

In reaction to these conditions, some questions are in order. All of these conditions affect how people learn, so shouldn't everybody think about them? If your students are going to be teachers, shouldn't they be in the habit of considering what the best conditions for learning are? Of course, the answers to these questions are all yes. And that is the problem. You are likely teaching in a traditional school that does not ask teachers or students to reflect on many issues, many more than were mentioned above.

THINKING AND ASKING QUESTIONS NOW IS GOOD PREPARATION FOR BECOMING A TEACHER LATER

Is *not* thinking about these questions good for your students' preparation as teachers, or would it be better for everyone to be asking questions about our traditional way of doing things to determine if they are still the best way to do things? As a teacher of aspiring teachers, ask yourself right now if you think students and teachers should be thinking about and asking questions about how our schools are designed and whether or not we should change them.

Then ask yourself this: Would it be good preparation for aspiring teachers to ask these questions now and talk about them with their teachers while their teachers are still available to them?

Teachers of future teachers should consider encouraging their students to go to their teachers and say, "I'm thinking about becoming a teacher, and I would like to discuss some things. I want to tell you about how I experience school, what I really get out of it, and what I think we need to do to change and make it better. And I want to know how you respond." Doing this, students can begin to drive the evolution of learning, and they will become better prepared to be teachers.

RESEARCHERS MADE DISCOVERIES BY LISTENING TO STUDENTS

The author is a career secondary school teacher and an educational researcher, and he has focused his research on how secondary school students explain their experience of secondary school. "How students experience secondary school" means trying to understand how students feel about what they do every day at school and how they *really* think about and respond to it. So, in order to understand how students experience secondary school, he interviewed the students themselves and listened to their voices.

He asked students to tell about what it is like to be a secondary school student and to describe how they felt about it. The students explained that secondary school was all about doing what other people want them to do, doing it the way they want them to do it and when they want them to do it. Students made it clear that nearly all of the classes a student takes are required either by the local board of education, the state, the federal government, or by the fact that a student wants to go to college.

The students interviewed during the research said that they wanted more choices, and they wanted to be able to spend more time on learning about things that *they* wanted to learn about. They said that secondary school had so many requirements that doing everything that was required made them sometimes feel like "slaves" or "prisoners." Most of them said that they did the work they had to do in secondary school just so they could "get it over with" so then they could get to things that they enjoyed doing or really wanted to learn (Waters, 2012).

Of course, to have such choices, the school leaders and teachers would have to listen to students and find out what their interests are. The problem is that listening to what students have to say about learning and teaching is not part of traditional schooling. In a traditional secondary school, students are just supposed to do what the adults think is best for them. You may or may not share these perceptions, but the most important question is: Do you think it is the right thing to do to really listen to students? Moreover, should the aspiring teachers you are teaching be coached to think that in the future, listening to students will be important work for teachers?

LISTENING TO STUDENTS MAKES LEARNING MORE MEANINGFUL

Then, consider this: Some research has been done with listening to the voices of recent secondary school graduates. College freshman were asked about what they thought their most meaningful learning was in secondary school. None of them mentioned any of their academic classes. None. All of them said it was an extracurricular activity like participation in a play, a club, or becoming a member of a team or something entirely outside of school like writing a blog, creating video games, or supporting a clean water project. Think about it. None claimed their most meaningful learning was in an academic class (Byrnes, 2005). What does that mean? What does it mean for students as future teachers?

Now it is time for you and your students to ask yourselves the same question. When you stop to think about it, what was or has been your most meaningful learning experience in secondary school? (And it is okay if it *is* in an academic class.) This is an important question for teachers of aspiring teachers to think about. What makes learning "meaningful"? Will your students be teachers who make learning meaningful?

The point is that there seems to be a pattern. Students found that their most meaningful learning experiences were in classes or projects where they had some choice, when their preferences were listened to. And you know what? Students also said they worked much harder in classes or extracurricular activities that they chose for themselves or in projects they chose for themselves outside of school just because they enjoyed doing them (Childress, 2000; Cushman, 2010; Damon, 2008; Waters, 2012).

In fact, nearly all of the out-of-school projects that students chose for themselves were complicated, time consuming, and very educational. When students make such choices, it shows that they are not lazy. It shows that choice and ownership are important parts of real learning. It also shows that when students are listened to, they can provide important insights about what really goes on in secondary school.

The point of this chapter is that students are important members of their schools and that they should be invited to voice their ideas to influence how and what they learn and how the school is run. This will be particularly true for your students as they prepare to become teachers. They should be thinking of themselves as thinkers and decision makers who want to fully participate in the creation of a school where students are engaged in authentic learning, not grade grubbing to satisfy others.

There is, in fact, research from secondary schools that shows that when students think about what and how they learn or how their teachers should teach, it is helpful to students. It supports their maturity (Joselowsky, 2007). The research also found that students believed that when the teachers and school leaders really listened to them, it helped students learn (Cook-Sather, 2002, 2006; Holcomb, 2007; Joselowsky, 2007; Mitra, 2004). The problem was that students were also skeptical that adults would make changes based on what students said (Yazzie-Mintz, 2009).

LEARNING COMMUNITIES NEED DIVERSITY

The whole idea of a learning community is about people listening to one another. Forming a learning community suggests the desire to hear from many and diverse perspectives. The learning community concept affirms the notion that good ideas and actions come from people with a variety of vantage points putting their heads together. Unfortunately, sometimes learning communities can lack diversity. If a learning community is made up of similar people from similar backgrounds with similar frames of reference, the lack of diversity stands to diminish the whole purpose of a learning community.

As a teacher of aspiring teachers, you are encouraged to get your students thinking about a few things in this regard. First, they should consider their own response as students to the prospect of being invited by teachers to share their voices and become part of the learning community. They probably feel, "Well, it is about time." And they also probably feel quite sure that they could share some pretty important thoughts about school, learning, and instruction. In general, they would be happy to know that the adults had come to their senses and invited the students to express themselves.

If, now, your students look at their aspiring teacher program and their school as a whole, do they see that it is diverse and inclusive? Are there people or groups that are not represented, that have not been invited in? If they see that there are some people or groups that are not included, this presents a challenge to them and their learning community. It is a challenge faced by all contemporary educators. What can be done to make our learning communities more inclusive?

There are two ways in which this should be important to your students' aspiring teacher learning community. The first has to do with what is going on in their school now. The second has to do with what is going on in the teaching profession, itself, now and the future. In both cases, the primary question is whether or not everyone feels invited in to the learning community and the teaching profession.

WHAT IS THE STATE OF INCLUSION IN YOUR STUDENTS' SCHOOL?

Let's take a deeper look at your students' school. As aspiring teachers, when they take a careful look, do they see that not all students feel full membership in their school? Do they see this common scenario that typically takes place in our secondary schools: one kind of student that tends to occupy the positions of power and influence among students? These are students who get good grades and plan to go to college. They are students who are confident in expressing themselves and probably enjoy school. These students are likely student council members, club presidents, class presidents, and maybe the student council president. They may even be aspiring teachers.

Now look at all of the other students. Do your students think most of those other students share the feeling that "I have a voice" or "I have influence in my school?" Or, do most of those students feel voiceless as they do the things they feel forced to do at school? Do they have any sense that their opinions count or that they could influence events around school? The fact is that in almost every school, large numbers of students do not feel included. *These students will need to be invited in.*

Consider that many educational authorities have observed that our schools give good service to only about 30 percent of students. These are students who are good linguistic learners. They like books, reading, speaking out, and writing down their ideas. The other 70 percent don't see the school as their friend but rather a constant judge against which they rarely do well. These same students may enjoy learning in many other ways that are not linguistic but more interpersonal, physical, or hands-on. They may prefer to spend most of their hours learning in fields like music, art, cinema, dance, design, mechanics, drama, construction, athletics, and other areas.

Nearly 30 percent of all high school students in the United States drop out of school every year. Another large percentage becomes in-school dropouts who stay in school but do little and achieve little while they are there. As already discussed, many more go through high school just grubbing grades while making little personal investment in their learning. When your students become teachers, the creation of learning communities will make them responsible for inviting in and giving good service to students who are traditionally outsiders and feel school does not work for them. How can they be prepared for that challenge?

WHAT IS THE STATE OF INCLUSION IN THE TEACHING PROFESSION?

The teaching profession, itself, has a diversity problem. Like any local learning community, the teaching profession needs to invite more people in. The vast majority of teachers in the United States are white women. While their interest in education and its long history has been wonderful for American schools, the profession needs more minority membership.

This is true for a lot of reasons, but the most important is because it is membership, itself, that invites more minorities in. When minority students see more minority teachers, they know they are invited into the teaching profession. This invitation should include not only more minority women but also especially more men, white men, black men, and Hispanic men. All of these groups are poorly represented in the teaching profession.

As aspiring teachers tasked with forming their first learning community this year, how will your students get the ball rolling, this year, to become more diverse and representative of your school's community? Meeting this challenge of building a truly diverse learning community will prepare them for a future in teaching where the same challenge awaits.

EVERYBODY NEEDS TO BE INVITED IN, EVEN TEACHERS

When your students recognize the need to diversify their learning community, where and how can they begin? It's simple. Members of their learning community will have to reach out and start approaching other students and saying something like, "Have you ever thought about being a teacher? I would like to invite you to a meeting we are having for students who are thinking about becoming teachers. We think you would be a good candidate, and we would really like it if you would come."

Also remember that this doesn't have to happen just at school. It could happen in the neighborhood, at Scouts, your place of worship. While in-person invitations are probably best, they could be done on the phone or even on social media with a personal follow-up later. As students do this, have them keep in mind how much people like being invited in. It makes them feel special. Everyone likes feeling special.

Along with this invitation, it would be a good idea to have something written like a flyer that gives the time and date of the meeting. Mention that this is a "special invitation for . . . , and write the name of the invited student on the invitation. Also mention some yummy refreshments. Good meetings always include refreshments. In all of this, students should be mindful that their efforts stand to encourage other students to make terrifically positive, life-changing decisions, should they decide to become teachers.

CONCLUSION

This chapter has been about how listening to students stands to improve schools. Research has shown that listening to students' voices could have enormous impact, even changing what we think students should learn. Listening to students' voices points to a rejection of the one-size-fits-all approach to learning and points the way to a more individualized and customized kind of learning that draws on students' strengths, talents, and interest.

Will your students become teachers interested in listening to students, or will they mindlessly adhere to the traditional ways of doing things that schools have used for decades and that marginalize the voices of both students and teachers?

DISCUSSION QUESTIONS

1. What is the most convincing argument for listening to students?
2. How can students be prepared to speak up so they don't just complain but offer great suggestions for school improvement?

3. Do students understand the concept of token inclusion and how to avoid it?

LEADERSHIP ACTIVITIES

1. Make a list of times and places for students to speak out at school.
2. Arrange an event for students to speak out.

TEXTBOX 6.1. PUBLIC SCHOOL TEACHERS ARE LEADING THE WAY

Student Voice

In her book *Student Voice in School Reform: Building Youth-Adult Partnerships That Strengthen Schools and Empower Youth*, Dana L. Mitra (2008) tells the inspirational story of Whitman High School of the San Francisco Bay area. It is the story of a school that achieved significant reform driven by a belief that students had a meaningful role to play in clarifying the realities for students in their school and how to make the school better. Mitra explained,

> Rather than importing solutions [for reform] developed by outside organizations that presume to know how to fix schools, this line of thought suggested that teachers and administrators in schools process unique knowledge about their school's contexts. . . . In other words, actors within school examine their everyday realities to identify what needs to be fixed and how. (19)

This focus on teachers' unique knowledge then evolved to include that of students who were involved in not only responding to surveys but later "to analyze the focus group data of their peers. This work blossomed into students wanting to take action on the concerns they identified in the focus group transcripts" (Mitra, 2008, 23).

Consistent with the ideas developed in this book, Mitra also saw "the experience of Whitman High School raise important questions for how schools can broaden current conceptions of a school's learning community and decision-making processes" (71). Mitra's report is just one of many.

Chapter Seven

Teachers Facilitate Greater Individualization of Study

In the context of building professional learning communities, it has been established that listening to many perspectives is key. One of the likely outcomes of listening more to students would be that their teachers would learn more about the things students are interested in and want to learn. It may even give teachers insights into the circumstances under which students learn best. All of this is likely to lead to some effort to give students programs of study that are more individualized and customized to their unique talents, strengths, and passions.

The impulse to provide students more individualized learning is, in fact, supported by a great deal of research. A primer reference list of books about the benefits of individualized learning will be provided later in this chapter. It is important for you to help aspiring teachers understand that providing individualized learning is not just about being nice to students. It is about improving student learning.

You may find such individualization and customization hard to believe because in the school where you are currently teaching there are probably a lot of required classes and your students are used to taking such classes. In fact, generally around 85 percent of the classes secondary schools students take are required by local, state, or federal authorities or by the fact that they plan to go to colleges that require certain background subjects.

Demanding that students take these requirements is a part of secondary school that has been going on for a long time. People take it for granted that students need these required subjects for a variety of reasons. Recently, however, some educators have begun to challenge this thinking. Some have started to think that it would be more productive to educate youth around subjects for which they have a personal interest and are willing to give a strong effort instead of forcing them to take requirements.

To better understand this educational issue, let's think about all of the requirements that your students have to deal with in secondary school. All of these requirements come from decisions made by important people who work in local, state, and federal government offices. These important people think the schools have to make their students know all sorts of things that will help them be better citizens, better workers, or better college students. The truth is that most everything that they want students to know is pretty good stuff. It would be good for most people to know it. So, what is the problem?

The problem comes when you look at human nature. The reality is that not everybody wants to learn the same thing at the same time in the same way. Everybody is different. One student has certain interests. Their friend has different interests. Each goes about learning at different times, at different paces, and in different ways. It's human nature. The reality of human differences is a well-established concept. You probably see in yourself that your interests and ways of learning are different from your colleagues.

INDIVIDUALS CAUGHT IN BUREAUCRACY AND STANDARDIZATION

The problem gets worse when the important people in local, state, and federal governments find this simple fact of human variation to be inconvenient. The fact that every person is different makes things complicated and hard to control. So they ignore it. They ignore it in favor of doing things in schools so they can be standardized and more easily controlled and managed. These twentieth-century thinkers love *bureaucracy* and *standardization.*

It is, then, important to understand that bureaucracy means breaking things up into compartments or sections, sort of like the different classrooms in your secondary school or the different subject departments like math, English, and science, or even like the textbooks you use in your classes.

Students should also be helped to understand that standardization means everybody has to learn the same things, from the same book, then answer the same questions in the same way, and then everybody has to take the same important state test like it came down from God or something. When everybody is doing these things in the same way, they are much easier to monitor and control than if everybody is doing something different.

These ideas of bureaucracy and standardization were important concepts in the nineteenth and twentieth centuries. Like the author, before becoming a teacher, your teachers and school leaders probably graduated from bureaucratic and standardized secondary schools. They likely passed the concepts on to your generation. Bureaucracy and standardization is what they knew. It was in their bones. They thought of it as being organized. Unfortunately, in the area of education, this belief in the benefits of bureaucracy and standardization has persisted into the twenty-first century. You may think this way also.

When things *are not* bureaucratic or standardized, *it scares people!* They get upset. Things seem disorganized. When a new idea comes to them for changing schools, if it doesn't involve standardization and bureaucracy, they hate it and sabotage it (Sopovitz & Weinbaum, 2008; Kelly, McCain, & Jukes, 2009). They do whatever they can to get back to what they know, standardization and bureaucracy.

ARE REQUIREMENTS REALLY NECESSARY?

Every time a town, county, state, or the federal government comes up with a new requirement for students, they have the idea that students could not go through life successfully if they didn't have this certain knowledge or have this certain set of skills. The people who create all of these requirements really want students to be well prepared for work, college, and life.

As a teacher of prospective teachers, you are faced with educational questions. Is it really true that a student could not succeed without studying a certain requirement? At the same time, is it possible for a student to learn the requirement indirectly? Could a student learn a lot about English, science, history, or any other subject by studying a subject of personal interest like automobile design, the Civil War, local politics, or the dead fish in a nearby pond? In other words, do we always have to have all students studying the same subject at the same time while reading the same textbook and answering the same questions at the same time? Could learning be more individualized?

After you have reviewed the references on individualized instruction, you will see that many educators think standardization is the wrong approach to learning. People are different, and they all learn in their own ways. It is also obvious to the most casual observer that there are many successful people in the world who did not study many of the subjects that today are requirements.

There are obviously many successful people in the world who didn't have a second year of algebra, or didn't have the health unit on communicable diseases, or didn't read *Romeo and Juliet*, or don't know how the Civil War started. Yes, it would be good to know all of these things. But is it absolutely necessary that everybody learn them at the same time and in the same way? No.

You can also think of this in another way. One of the jobs of a school is to help students learn about how the world works. Twentieth-century bureaucrats think that this has to be done by classroom teaching of specific courses in history or biology or geometry or civics or any of the other common courses in schools. But the truth is that a person can learn about all of these subjects and more by pursuing answers to the questions students really have.

This might include student questions like where do clouds come from, or where does wealth come from, or where do diseases come from, or why do we have to go to school. The fact is that all human beings want to learn, but they all do NOT want to learn the same things at the same times in the same places.

Each person is unique, and schools should focus on developing that uniqueness. The universe and civilization thrives on and grows from variety and uniqueness in all things, including human personalities. The fact is that many schools already acknowledge the importance of individual differences and they let students pick a book for a book report or maybe choose a project topic. But they could do a lot more.

The question for aspiring teachers then becomes, Should we redesign schools so individualization is easier to facilitate? Or, Should schools continue to force students to learn the same things at the same time in the same way?

TEXTBOX 7.1. THE INDIVIDUALIZATION OF LEARNING: A PRIMER REFERENCE LIST

Armstrong, T. (2000). *In their own way: Discovering and encouraging your child's multiple intelligences.* New York: Putnam Penguin, Inc.

Armstrong, T. (2006). *The best schools: How human development research should inform educational practice.* Alexandria, VA: Association for Supervision and Curriculum Development.

Beaudoin, N. (2008). *A school for each student: Personalization in a climate of high expectations.* Larchmont, NY: Eye on Education.

Cordova, D. I., & Lepper, M. R. (1996). Intrinsic motivation and the process of learning: Beneficial effects of contextualization, personalization, and choice. *Journal of Educational Psychology 88*(4), 715–30.

Deci, E. L., & Ryan, R. M. (2008a). Facilitating optimal motivation and psychological well-being across life's domains. *Canadian Psychology 49*(1), 14–23.

Deci, E. L., & Ryan, R. M. (2008b). Self-determination theory: A macrotheory of human motivation, development, and health. *Canadian Psychology 49*(3), 182–85.

Deci, E., Vallerand, R. J., Pelletier, L. G., & Ryan, R. M. (1991). Motivation and education: The self-determination perspective. *Educational Psychologist 26*(3–4), 325–46.

Dewey, J. (2012). *Interest and effort in education.* Charleston, SC: Forgotten Books.

DiMartino, J., Clarke, J., & Wolk, D. (2003). *Personalized learning: Preparing secondary school students to create their futures.* Lanham, MD: Scarecrow Press, Inc.

Gardner, H. (2006). *Multiple intelligences: New horizons in theory and practice.* New York: Basic Books.

Gibbons, M. (2002). *The self-directed learning handbook: Challenging adolescent students to excel.* San Francisco, CA: Jossey-Bass.

Guay, F., & Ratelle, C. F. (2008). Optimal learning in optimal contexts: The role of self-determination in education. *Canadian Psychology 49*(3), 233–40.

Hess, F. M., & Manno, B., eds. (2011). *Customized schooling: Beyond whole-school reform.* Cambridge, MA: Harvard University Press.

Jaros, M., & Deakin-Crick, R. (2006). Personalizing learning in the post-mechanical age. *Journal of Curriculum Studies 39*(4), 423–40.

Levine, E. (2002). *One kid at a time: Big lessons from a small school.* New York: Teachers College Press.

Littky, D. (2004). *The big picture: Education is everyone's business.* Alexandria, VA: ASCD.

Nagel, D. (2009). Students as "free agent learners." *T.H.E. Journal.* April. Retrieved at https://thejournal.com/articles/2009/04/24/students-as-free-agent-learners.aspx.

Paige, R. (2009). Self-directed learning and the mind-set of successful entrepreneurial learning. *ATEA Journal*, Fall.

Pink, D. (2009). *Drive: The surprising truth about what motivates us.* New York: Riverhead Books.

Silver, D. (2005). *Drumming to the beat of different marchers, revised edition: Finding the rhythm for differentiated learning.* Chicago, IL: Incentive Publications.

Sousa, D. A., & Tomlinson, C. A. (2010). *Differentiation and the brain: How neuroscience supports the learner-friendly classroom.* Bloomington, IN: Solution Tree Press.

Sulo, B. (2007). *Activating the desire to learn.* Alexandria, VA: Association for Supervision and Curriculum Development.

Turville, J. (2007). *Differentiating by student interest: Strategies and lesson plans.* Larchmont, NY: Eye on Education.

STUDENTS AND TEACHERS AS INDIVIDUAL THINKERS

Everyone would probably agree that what *is* absolutely necessary is that students be encouraged to think about what they want to know and how they want to find it out. Secondary school students need to learn to make thoughtful decisions and choices about their learning. They need to take ownership of their learning. They can't do that if everything is required and predetermined by other people.

Everybody is different, and everybody needs to think about it and create their own learning path. Students taking ownership of their learning will be an important part of the evolution of learning and teaching. Whether you agree with this thinking or not, it is a question you will need to consider as a teacher. Should teachers put more emphasis on appealing to students' personal talents and interests?

Research in secondary schools by the author and other researchers has shown that students do not like all of these standardized requirements, especially the big tests. It gives students this sense of constantly being judged and forced to do things for which they have little or no interests. They feel as if they have no control over their own lives. And students have to do it all of the time, day after day. They hate it.

In this regard, it is notable that research has determined when students get into secondary school, their engagement falls sharply (Sheehy, 2013). Why? Students end up spending hours doing things in which they have no interest, and they learn very little. Usually students learn how to game school and learn things just for the test, and then they forget it. Your students probably know this is true. Students have all sorts of ways of pretending to learn. There will be more discussion of how students pretend to learn later.

THREE IMPORTANT POINTS

It is important that prospective teachers should know that there is another way to look at learning. Everybody is different, and people like to be known and treated as individuals. Society now has the capacity to provide each student a highly individualized and customized educational experience (Hess & Manno, 2011). It is time that secondary schools started providing such learning opportunities, and students need to know that now is the time.

There is a great deal of research that supports the value of individualization. One strand of research shows that there are three things people must have.

1. *People need to believe that they are in charge of their own behavior.* They like choices, and they like making their own decisions. The older a person gets, the more he or she wants to be in charge of herself or himself. A twenty-first-century secondary school would work on this principle. Students would have a lot more choices, and they could create a schedule of learning that was customized for them. Unfortunately in most secondary schools today, it's all about requirements.
2. *People like to be connected to and supported by other people.* Students don't like it when they are not treated like thinking individuals by teachers and school leaders. They feel their individuality and their ability to make good decisions is not being recognized or respected. So then they feel as if adults who are important to them do not support them. And when they don't feel that support for their individuality, they begin to resist and subvert.

    Also, schools often keep students apart so they can't connect with each other. Students complain that they have to sit by themselves all day in single lecture desks (No talking, please!).
3. *People like to be competent.* This means that they enjoy the challenge of learning and the feeling of getting better and better at stuff. Of course, that gets really hard to feel if you have to work on topics all day in which you have little interest. Very often your teacher doesn't even know what your strong points are, and most students find them-

selves focused on their weak points most of the day. (Deci, 1995; Deci & Ryan, 1985, 2008a, 2008b; Deci et al., 1991; Reeve et al., 2002; Ryan & Deci, 2000, 2006).

It is probably hard to believe that teachers and school leaders have overlooked this research or don't understand these simple aspects of human nature. Whatever the reason, they have done little to build these concepts into contemporary schools. All they seem to be able to do is think up new requirements and ways to make everybody learn in the same way at the same time and get tested on the same material at the same level.

Just look at your school. When there is a lesson, there is one lesson for everybody. When there is homework, everybody has the same assignment. When there is a test, everybody has the same test. The fact is that if your students were to ask their teachers if they believed that every person is a unique individual, they would certainly say "yes." If they then asked their teachers, "Then why do you make everyone learn the same material in the same way at the same time?" their teachers would then hesitate and say, "Because it would be impossible or unrealistic to give everybody their own material, homework, or test."

When school leaders say things like this, it is twentieth-century thinking. It shows a belief in standardization. Another problem with that response is that it is not true. Society now has the capacity to give each student a highly individualized and customized learning plan, and there are, already, schools that have highly individualized and customized programs for their students. Hess and Manno in their 2011 work *Customized Schooling: Beyond Whole-School Reform* nicely develop the viability of such individualization.

CONCLUSION

This chapter has been about individualization as a benchmark of progress in the evolution of teaching and creating better schools. Students are not all the same, and they don't all want to learn the same things at the same time in the same way. You might be interested to know that recently a talented seventeen-year-old named Nikhil Goyal (2012) wrote a book about this very subject, titled *One Size Does Not Fit All: A Student's Assessment of School*. This book has been endorsed by many prominent educators and is recommended to all secondary school students, especially those who are thinking about becoming teachers. Both the book and Nikhil Goyal's presentations on YouTube give an insider's perspective on how a student experiences secondary school and the need for more individualization.

DISCUSSION QUESTIONS

1. Explain why you believe that there should be more individualization, or do you think having everybody studying the same subjects in the same way is a better idea? Why?
2. Could you explain to your group all of the things you could learn from studying a topic of personal interest?

LEADERSHIP ACTIVITY

Conduct a survey of students to find out what unique subjects they would like to study at school.

TEXTBOX 7.2. PUBLIC SCHOOL TEACHERS ARE LEADING THE WAY: INDIVIDUALIZATION

Avalon High School

Avalon High School is highlighted in the recent work *Deeper Learning: How Eight Innovative Public Schools Are Transforming Education in the Twenty-First Century* (Martinez & McGrath, 2014). The authors explain, "What all of our schools have in common is that they are reimagining how teachers teach and students learn. In each of them, teachers collaborate far more than the norm, supporting each other and jointly taking responsibility for the students' success. In each, as well, the bottom-line is to help students become more engaged in and responsible for their own learning" (14).

The focus on individualization as part of deep learning is captured in the school orientation program called Project Brainstorm, where teachers ask new students to think about "What do you want to learn? What would you like to do better? What are you good at?" and "What do you know?" (23)

These questions prepare students for a very different schooling experience where teachers call themselves advisors, students help other students, and upperclassmen are eager to mentor incoming freshmen. It all supports the "belief that developing students into self-directed, responsible learners concerned for the learning of others is a fundamental requirement for Deeper Learning" (25).

Martinez and McGrath explain that as a learning community, "the teacher run Avalon School doesn't even have a principal. There, teachers commonly take on duties many traditional principals handle themselves, such as hiring, creating schools schedules, developing partnerships with off-campus corporations and museums, and even dealing with funders. Furthermore, unlike at most traditional schools, these teachers direct their own professional development, identifying issues of common concern, planning workshops, and helping each other adapt to new technology" (42).

Chapter Eight

Teachers Investigate Students' Learning Engagement

When your students think about becoming teachers, they are likely inspired by you or some of the great teachers they have now or have had in the past. These teachers probably made learning in their classes interesting, maybe even exciting. On top of that, these teachers probably were pleasant to work with as people and may have touched and inspired your students in personal ways. In the overall, something about these teachers moved students to also consider becoming teachers. Even you, now a teacher of aspiring teachers, may look back on your own journey and see that there were special teachers who had a powerful influence on you.

If these teachers have influenced you and your students to consider being teachers, they have, indeed, had a very positive impact. Your students will probably carry their inspiration forward into their own careers and inspire even more students themselves. In so doing, they are headed toward a career of helping and inspiring young people where they stand to enjoy very profound rewards that may be associated with the deepest and most meaningful aspects of human life.

In spite of this positive influence, research in secondary schools indicates that most students, most of the time, do not enjoy the same level of inspiration that you and your students have enjoyed (Yazzie-Mintz, 2009; Sheehy, 2013). In fact, the same research indicates that student engagement falls off radically in secondary school and large numbers of students are actually bored during much of their school day (Busteed, 2014; Sheehy, 2013; Yazzie-Mintz, 2007, 2009). You have probably experienced such boredom yourself in your own schooling.

When you consider your own work as a teacher, you have probably made up your mind that you are not going to be a boring teacher. This chapter has to do with understanding how students respond to the work they have to do in school and how engaged they feel when they do all the things they do in school. In other words, it has to do with getting students interested, not bored. Based on the cited research, schools have a lot of work to do to improve in this area. Your leadership and the leadership of your students are needed.

PAY ATTENTION TO STUDENT ENGAGEMENT

The term *student engagement* means how fully involved students are when they do the things they have to do at school. Being fully engaged would be like if you really enjoyed what you are doing, you felt it was fun or exciting, you found yourself really concentrating but with little effort, you didn't want to be interrupted by the bell, and you felt as if the activity had a lot of meaning for you personally; that is, your head and your heart were really in it.

Take a moment now just to recall a time when you felt really engaged. It could be a time when you were in school or a time out of school, a time when you were doing something that you loved doing, you learned a lot, time flew by, and you didn't find yourself day dreaming or wanting to do other things.

Now, think about this: Did the following ever happen to you as a student? Your teacher or an administrator told you that the adults wanted to find out how engaged you were at school; that is, they wanted to find out about your inner experience at school, if you and other students really liked, enjoyed, got deeply involved with, and felt as if they were learning a lot from the things done at school.

There are a few schools that do this, but very few. Did your school do it when you were a student? Does the school you teach in now do it? If not, why do you think your school leaders don't do it? Wouldn't it make sense for the adults to find out whether or not students are enjoying and really learning in all of the programs they provide? The community is spending a lot of money on your school.

Or, is it possible that your school leaders never thought of asking? After all, no one asked them when they were in secondary school in the twentieth century. Or, is it possible that they don't want to know? Does asking students about how they experience secondary school and if they are really learning sound like a good idea to you? Why wouldn't the value of such an idea be apparent to your school leaders?

WORKING HARD, NOT LEARNING DEEPLY

As you consider these questions, you should remember that even students who get good grades are often not learning deeply. We all know there are ways to learn things for tests and get good grades even though we can't remember what we learned two weeks later. If this is true, why don't teachers and school leaders try to find out if students are really engaged and really learning in a deep way at school?

As you guide your students, you should ask them to look around at the other students and consider all of the things students do to get through secondary school. If they look at all of their behaviors, they may realize that a lot of what students do has nothing to do with learning. They have to do with making teachers and parents happy even though they are not learning very much. Many students are not really engaged.

Let's face it, just because a student is in school does not mean that that is where his or her thoughts are. Every human being has a way of "checking out" if faced with doing something that they do not enjoy even if the experience might be good for them. Everybody knows that it does not matter how hard the teacher is working, if the student is not engaged, then little will be learned.

And consider this: Research has shown that even a lot of the kids who get good grades are not doing it because they love learning. They are doing it just for the grades or to get approval from their parents, teachers, or other students (Ames & Archer, 1988; Fredricks et al., 2004). But after those students get that grade, what do they do? They usually forget almost everything. They don't say, "Oh, I loved that subject and I want to study it more."

The truth is that even good students are often disengaged. They are doing what they have to do at school because they have to do it, no other reason. They do it because they want to satisfy their parents, their teachers, their friends, and they want to get into a good college. They don't do it because they have learned to love learning. If you have never seen the fine film *Race to Nowhere* (Abelese & Congdon, 2009), among other things in education, it illustrates the stressful work students commit to for reasons of achievement and competition without making a personal investment in learning.

The point here is that even though teachers investigating student engagement is not currently something that happens in traditional schools, it should be happening. And the next generation of teachers should know that if they really want to advance the profession of teaching, they should undertake the work to find out the level of student engagement in their schools.

The point of view of this book is that the students' point of view is important. Students know what it is at school that makes them want to learn and what does not. With that kind of insight, the adults should want to know what the students think. The adults should be asking students to tell them about how they experience school. They should ask students how they are enjoying school, how engaged they really are, and how much they think they are learning.

The adults should do this because *if your students are really engaged, then they are learning.* If they are not fully engaged, then they are probably learning very little or just going through the motions so it looks like they are being a good student. University researchers have come up with a lot of different ways to find out about how engaged students really are. Below is one example you and your students might consider. Try it out.

ACTIVITY

Read the following five statements in the "Engagement Continuum." Rewrite one of the statements so it expresses how *you* experience each of the classes in your current secondary school schedule. For example, maybe you feel that number 1 comes close to expressing how you experience three of your current classes. So, you would rewrite number 1 so it comes as close as possible to expressing how you experience those three classes. Write a statement that reflects the different levels of engagement you feel for all of your different classes. Feel free to borrow phrases or sentences from other levels or make up your descriptions.

Engagement Continuum

1. I'm deeply involved in what I do in this class. I actually enjoy the work. I feel happy when I'm doing it. Time flies by. I have a strong sense of having learned a lot. I can see the value it has for my life today and that it is meaningful in terms of what really matters to me in life-long terms.
2. I put on my game face and show a positive attitude in this class, but I don't feel the work has meaning for me personally, and I don't see how it is relevant to my life today. When I do the work, I feel as if I just want to do what I'm supposed to do and get it over with. However, I know people think the different subjects are important so I do what I have to do to get the grades that I need. I like getting good grades so I will work pretty hard in a class even if I don't love the subject or the work that is assigned.
3. I pretty much do what the teacher says we have to do because I don't want to fail. When I do the work I feel frustrated and even a little angry, but I know what I have to do. I'm a fairly smart student so I can pretty much pass my classes without working myself too hard. Although I have other interests, there is very little in the work in this

class that makes me interested enough that I would really want to work on it.
4. I do close to nothing in this class. I hardly even listen because I would rather think about or do other things like text, read a book, write notes to my friends, day dream, or sleep if I'm allowed. Just being in school makes me mad and I feel trapped. I never disrupt or distract the class, but I do think about it.
5. I hate the work, and I usually don't do it, and I don't care if I fail. I usually do what I want like talk to my friends, text, make weird noises, throw things, tease people I don't like, and argue with the teacher. I feel schoolwork is stupid, and I hate it. I like it when things go wrong like fire drills, fights, bomb scares, teacher absences, and technology breakdowns. To me the other students are kiss ups who are well behaved because they are afraid, not because they love schoolwork. (Waters, 2012)

Okay, so now you and your students may have a little better idea about how students experience what they do at school. There are no right answers to this activity. Everybody feels and experiences things differently. Neither you nor your students should worry about being judged for what they think or have written down.

Now, do you think it would be a good idea for the adults to know how students feel about and experience secondary school? What could they do with that information? Would it help them make a better school? Hmm, so why don't teachers and school leaders try to find out this information? It makes you think, right? Will your students want to know what students think when they become teachers?

Certainly your students have had a teacher or two over the years who has asked students to evaluate their classes. The students probably felt pretty good knowing that the teacher was interested in their point of view. Wouldn't it be a good idea for teachers and school leaders to try to better understand how students experience school by asking them directly? That is the point of view of this book.

CONCLUSION

This chapter has dealt with a concept in learning that is getting more and more attention, student engagement. Because we know that students are not really learning when they are not engaged, teachers and school leaders need to pay more attention to student engagement by asking students about it and planning learning experiences with a high priority placed on eliciting student engagement.

DISCUSSION QUESTIONS

1. Explain why you agree or disagree with the idea that adults understanding student engagement is important.
2. Explain why you believe students in your school do or do not feel safe discussing their real levels of engagement with teachers.

LEADERSHIP ACTIVITY

Form a committee and talk to your school leaders about conducting a school engagement survey at your school. There are many free surveys available, such as the High School Survey of Student Engagement from Indiana University.

TEXTBOX 8.1. PUBLIC SCHOOL TEACHERS ARE LEADING THE WAY

Student Engagement

Teachers at Black Hills High School in Washington State have led the way in focusing on student engagement by creating a Student Engagement Team (SET). A report in the journal *Northwest Education* explains,

> It started with the formation of a student engagement team (SET) in 2005. The group met weekly before school with social studies teacher Carole Layton acting as the advisor and gently guiding force. Layton views SET as "an opportunity for me to model democracy and teach citizenship." She says, "This is what grass roots is all about. [SET members] understand how bottom up works." Shalom, an SET activist, adds, "This gives you insight and experience you can use in the community as an adult, more than your basic book education. We are the decision makers [*sic*] of tomorrow." In a neon yellow promotional brochure, SET describes itself as an organization that "brings together students who want to learn more about how school works, and how students and adults can work together in partnership to improve on an ongoing basis." Since its formation, the Black Hills High School SET has written a manual on how to start a student engagement team, conducted schoolwide student and faculty surveys, and testified before the Washington State House of Representatives Education Committee. The team drafted a strategic plan for the State of Washington that explains

why student engagement is important. It asserts: "Students who are involved in their own learning care more about education and do better in school and life." (32–33 [Spring–Summer 2008] *13*[3])

Chapter Nine

Teachers Elicit Intrinsic Motivation and "Knowing Myself as a Learner"

Your students' decisions to become teachers are likely based on some things they know about themselves. Most probably they see in themselves some special enthusiasm for a particular subject and/or age group. They also likely find in themselves a disposition of caring about others, of wanting to help young people. No one told them that they must be interested in the subjects they love, and nobody demanded that they must enjoy helping young people. Each student just feels the desire to pursue these areas as a part of who they are. It's what each wants to do.

Such motivation is called intrinsic motivation. That is, a person is motivated to get involved in certain areas of life just because she or he finds them appealing for personal reasons of interest, challenge, or enjoyment. It is not required. There is no motivation to get rewards or any kind of compensation. A person just enjoys the activity.

As a result of this intrinsic motivation and your knowledge of it, you undertook all of the challenges of becoming a teacher. Now you are teaching aspiring teachers who are considering becoming teachers and also undertaking all of the study and preparation that goes with that. Now, your students have made some decisions about their futures and how to guide their educations so they will be well prepared for their careers as teachers. In effect, they are guiding the course of their educations based on their knowledge of their unique characteristics as learners.

This chapter develops the logic of building a young person's learning around their intrinsic motivation and their unique characteristics as learners as opposed to a one-size-fits-all approach, which is what most schools offer their students. When teachers begin to focus on eliciting students' intrinsic motivation based on knowledge of themselves as learners, that will be an important benchmark in the evolution of teaching.

INTRINSIC MOTIVATION

Everyone has intrinsic motivation. If you look at yourself, you can probably see that there are some things that you do just because you want to, not because you are going to get some kind of a reward for doing it. This could be anything from collecting certain music, writing in a journal, reading books, or collecting old hubcaps.

It could be anything at all. In fact, the world is an interesting place because there are so many people with unique, odd, or even weird interests. The fact is, our civilization needs to have people with a broad range of interests. So your students should know that if their interests are unusual, even weird, they shouldn't be embarrassed because the world needs them!

Research has shown that many teenagers have some kind of learning project that they pursue for no other reason except that they like doing it (Childress, 2000; Cushman, 2010; Damon, 2008; Waters, 2012). Sometimes these projects are for school, such as joining a team or club or collecting shells for a science class, or outside of school, such as helping at a day care center, writing a blog, or learning to handle a therapy dog for work with small children.

As you look at your own work as a teacher at school, you are probably aware of things you teach for which you have some intrinsic motivation. It was probably also true for you as a student that in some of your classes you felt intrinsically motivated to do some of the work. You just enjoyed the topics or the activities. In other classes you may have had no intrinsic motivation. In these classes you probably needed some kind of reward to do what is required of you. So at school students are offered grades, credits, and promotions for doing the things that they would not do otherwise.

Of course, the big problem at school is that nearly everything students have to do requires some possible rewards or punishments because otherwise students wouldn't do them. One of the reasons this is a problem is that when students are constantly doing things for rewards, sometimes they can lose sight of what they really want to do and what their real interests are. Or, they can begin to think that the things in which they are interested are not as important as the things they are taught in school.

One of the issues your students have to face as aspiring teachers is the role of intrinsic motivation and its relationship to the many requirements they have in schools. More specifically, do all the requirements that schools have push students' intrinsic motivation out of the way?

One of the students who participated in the research for this book loved working with children, but at school there was no course in child psychology, no course in childhood learning, no course in how to develop good character in children, and no provision for independent study. The student said she would have loved to have such courses, but the school didn't offer them, and there really wasn't room in her schedule anyway (Waters, 2012).

Because she was so highly motivated, this student could have learned a lot about vocabulary, reading, statistics, history, science, and psychology if she had been allowed to take an online course, an independent study course, a county college course, a group-reading independent study course, an apprenticeship, or was allowed to invent her own course. But, no, that wasn't possible because her school did not employ such alternative paths to learning. On top of that, there wasn't room in her schedule because of so many requirements.

Another young woman who participated in the research loved working with animals. She volunteered at a local center that helped injured animals, but at school, there were no courses in which she could develop her deep interest in helping animals. Another student had learned to work with therapy dogs in helping children to read. The thing was, at school there was no way to develop this interest in the relationship between animals and human emotions (Waters, 2012).

This student would have loved to have had classes about animals, but the school just didn't offer anything. The good news is that these students and others continued to spend many hours after school and on weekends working with these projects that had captured their passions. But they were not assisted by their school, and they received no credit for what they did. Your students should be asked to consider this current condition in our secondary schools and also asked to propose solutions. That will be part of their work as teachers in the future.

The point of this information is that, again, we can see that our schools, which were designed by adults about one hundred years ago, don't leave much room for the unique interests that students always have. When students have these interests, there is always a lot of energy attached to them. Students show a lot of dedication (Childress, 2000; Cushman, 2010; Damon, 2008; Waters, 2012).

The problem is that all of the requirements at school and the failure of schools to recognize alternative paths in learning make it nearly impossible for students to follow their personal interests. With this in mind, it would be good for your students to reflect on their own personal interests and passions. Consider having them complete the exercise below.

Assuming your students have considered some of the prompts in this exercise, they should be asked these questions: Do your teachers ever ask you about your unique qualities as a learner? Should teachers know about

Knowing Myself as a Learner

By

_____(Your Name)_____

Over the years I have learned that my strengths as a learner are

I know I have a special strength in _____ because

I also know that I am weak in

People have told me I have a talent for

My most recent high-engagement learning experience was

What I liked about it was

I am a very unique person because of my strong interest in

I get bored when

At this stage of my life, I find my greatest interest is in

At this stage of my life, I am strongly considering _____ as a career

In one class, I am hoping to learn

Possibly to do so projects involving

I've always wished I had more opportunities to learn about

I might be able to make a unique contribution to a class by

The thing I will probably need a lot of help with at school is
(Waters, 2012)

Figure 9.1.

your unique qualities as a learner? Would you enjoy school more if you thought your teachers really knew and understood you and you were able to focus more on topics that really interested you?

Of course, answering these questions for themselves as students eventually leads you to answering these questions as aspiring teachers. Should teachers know more about their students and allow that to influence a more personalized and customized approach to learning? Would such individualization allow for greater expression of intrinsic motivation and all of the energy that goes with it?

As your students consider these questions, they probably see that their uniqueness as a person has a big influence on how they learn at school. So why don't teachers spend more time trying to understand their students as individuals before they start teaching them?

STANDARDIZATION AGAIN

The answer to this question brings us, again, to the idea of standardization. Many school leaders and teachers believe that it is their job to provide all students with the same information and skills regardless of individual differences. That's why nearly everybody takes the same courses like English, math, history, science, and so on. And in those classes everybody gets the same textbook and does the same work from that book.

So, as aspiring teachers, your students are faced with a dilemma. On the one hand the adults at school are telling students that in order to be successful in the world, they need to study all of the required material that is offered in the courses at school. This one-size-fits-all approach is a long-standing tradition in almost all schools. In fact, more and more required courses are being added all the time.

On the other hand, this book has presented research suggesting that students' intrinsic motivation plays an important role in their learning and personal development. Because of the extra energy students bring to intrinsically motivated work, they could probably master many of the traditional subjects like reading, writing, history, science, and math by utilizing their strengths and following their learning passions.

A person can learn to love science by reading a novel, and a person could appreciate a poem by looking into a microscope. In other words, there are many pathways to learning what we need to know to be successful. It doesn't have to be the standardized way where every student does the same thing at the same time in the same way.

What could make your students' dilemma as prospective teachers even more difficult is the conclusion of many researchers that their personal learning passions are not only as important as what they teach at school but are more important. And if they were allowed or helped to follow them, they would be better prepared for life than a student who just studied all of the conventional required stuff because he wanted high grades or to please his peers and parents.

CONCLUSION

This chapter has focused on important concepts in the psychology of learning, intrinsic motivation and self-knowledge. Students demonstrate intrinsic motivation when they do and learn things just because they enjoy them, not because they are going to get some kind of reward for it. Research has shown that the intrinsic motivation of teenagers often leads them to undertake demanding, complicated, and very educational pursuits in and outside of school.

DISCUSSION QUESTIONS

1. Why should teachers focus more on helping students understand themselves as learners?
2. Why should teachers make an effort to get a deep understanding of each student as a learner?
3. Should teachers focus more on eliciting intrinsic motivation in students?

LEADERSHIP ACTIVITIES

1. Conduct a survey in which students are asked about their intrinsically motivated learning.
2. Discuss with your teachers what they think about the importance of students understanding their unique qualities as learners.

TEXTBOX 9.1. PUBLIC SCHOOL TEACHERS ARE LEADING THE WAY

Intrinsic Motivation

The Castle View High School Mosaic Collective is a school that looks to capitalize on students' intrinsic desire to learn. A teacher captures in the following description the school's desire to depart from memory-based learning and recitation and involve students in learning what they want to learn:

Born in 2014 out of experience, frustration, curiosity, and a sense of educational righteousness, the Mosaic Collective is a project-based, problem-based, inquiry-based, and challenge-based learning environment housed in a traditional public high school. All together, we are a student-based learning program housed in a traditional public high school. All together, we are a student-based learning program that trades the bureaucratic distractions of the school factory and misguided over-reliance on content for the bliss of intrinsic learning and a strong focus on the needs of our students. As teachers in Mosaic we embrace our new roles. Our work is interdisciplinary, purposeful, and always challenging. We employ methods of design thinking to continuously iterate and evolve our ideas and practices. We work with and along side our students to build a true collective of learners. The Mosaic Collective does not grade nor does it adhere to traditional bell schedules. It empowers, trusts, creates and contributes while honoring interests, passions, and dreams—of both students and teachers alike. (cvmosaic.org/new-index-4#newpage-2)

Chapter Ten

Teachers Stop the Game of School

As secondary school students, your students have probably observed and thought about how school can be like a game. Many secondary school students have said they believe it is. In the course of the author's research (Waters, 2012), students explained that the game of school is about creating the appearance that you are doing what you are supposed to do at school even though you are not really learning.

The basic idea is that when students go to school they don't really go because they want to learn what is in the curriculum. Still, most students know that they have to behave and get good grades or they will disappoint their parents, their friends, and other people they care about. As one student explained it, "Kids do what they have to do to get good grades, get the respect of their friends, and to keep their parents happy. It's not because they love doing schoolwork." So, as it has been explained by Marge Sherer, executive editor of *Educational Leadership*, students "pretend school" (Sherer, 2008, 7).

Students make it look as if they are being good students *by creating the appearance of doing what they are supposed to* even when they are not. You probably know how it works. During recent research, students gave the following examples of how to game school.

- Instead of reading a book, ask a friend what was the book about.
- Write answers on your hand for a short answer test.
- Don't take the work home. Just do the homework in the morning or copy off another student.
- Students gang up to convince the teacher to change the date of the test, and they all promise that they will get an A on the test.
- Instead of reading a book, go to SparkNotes or Cliffs Notes.

- Use Google to get book summaries or write reports.
- Ask a friend for answers before the test.
- Have everybody say they don't understand when the teacher announces a test.
- Say "I'm sick" on the day of the test or when a paper is due.
- Say to the teacher "I don't get it" or "You didn't teach us this."
- Keep asking the teacher for a lot of help so you really don't have to work yourself.
- For a research paper, copy someone else's paper and paraphrase.
- Everyone ask the teacher to delay an assignment.
- Make friends with someone who will let you copy homework.
- If you're assigned a research paper and you don't want to do it, put it off for as long as possible or try to get a college student to give you a paper.
- Download a research paper from the Internet.
- Have somebody else take your SATs. (Waters, 2012)

Certainly you are aware that students do these things, but you may never have thought of how gamelike it is.

Student explanations went something like this. The game of school is about creating false appearances: I did the homework when I didn't; I wrote the paper when I didn't; I discussed the book we were assigned but I really read the SparkNotes, not the book; I appeared to be taking notes from the lesson, but, no, I was actually writing a note to my friend; I'm looking the teacher in the eyes as if I were listening, but, really, I am day dreaming and planning what I'm going to do after school.

The game of school is all about appearances. It's all about appearing to do what one is told to do—learn—without really doing what one is told to do—learn.

Let's say a student is sitting in a class and her teacher is presenting a lesson. Most students understand that they have to look like they are paying attention. But are they really? Students revealed during research that more often than not they are

> texting
> watching the clock
> day dreaming
> doodling
> writing notes to friends
> going on Facebook or thinking about it
> planning for after school
> whispering to a friend
> doing homework for another class
> admiring another student

thinking about my life (Waters, 2012)

Certainly reading about what these students have said is probably not a surprise to you. It is part of everyday life in most secondary schools. So the game of school is about creating false appearances. It includes all of the cheating, lying about homework, test and paper delaying tactics, absenteeism, bathroom going, homework copying, Internet downloading of papers, and all of the rest.

When one stops to think of it, the game of school is a strong indication that most students are not deeply engaged in what they are doing at school. They are only faking it. They are only playing the game of school. Some students said that in the game of school what you learn doesn't really matter. What matters is that you appear to do what you are supposed to do. And these are two different things.

Students explained that if you do what you are told, you will get credit for the assignment or course. If two weeks after the course you have no interest in the subject and can't remember a thing, it doesn't matter. You got the credits because you did what you were told to do. Let's face it. We can all remember classes in secondary school that we passed but a short time later we could not remember what we learned.

Now think of it in this way. Schools cost millions and millions of dollars to run, maybe tens of millions. And if most of the students are just pretending to be students, what are we spending all of the money on? Or, think of it in this way. If most students are only playing the game of school, would it be a good idea to stop and think about how schools could change so kids really wanted to learn? This big question is one your students will have to face as aspiring teachers. Is there anything we can do to stop the game of school?

WHAT WILL YOUR STUDENTS' OUTLOOK BE AS TEACHERS?

But in order to do that, the adults would have to take time to ask the students how they really experience secondary school. If students really told them the truth, it would probably make all of the adults feel bad, like they weren't doing such a good job. Do you think that the adults might be avoiding facing that reality? Do they just want to keep doing business as usual?

Dealing with this condition is, of course, an opportunity for leadership. It is a tough issue that few educators want to face. Large numbers of students in secondary schools are not engaged in a meaningful way (Yazzie-Mintz, 2009; Busteed, 2013). They are just gaming their way through school. Add to this that there is an increasing body of research that suggests students continue this gaming strategy through their college years (Bain, 2012; Deresiewicz, 2015).

As prospective teachers who are still in secondary school, your students are positioned better than most to face this situation. As students, they know how to play the game of school. They understand that it is about cheap learning. As aspiring teachers, they probably don't like the game of school because they know it would cheapen their efforts as teachers to help youth. That's not what their career dreams are about.

ADULTS PLAY THE GAME OF SCHOOL, TOO

Now comes some really difficult information. The adults play the game of school, too. Like students, the adults in most schools perform their own gaming behavior by trying to create the appearance of compliance with the power structure with which they have to deal. This includes superintendents, local boards of education, and, especially, federal and state requirements on which funding is based.

So just like students, school leaders focus on the things for which they get credit, whether or not students are learning. These evaluation points include an orderly school, good daily attendance, a large number of AP or Baccalaureate classes, a high graduation rate, a strong focus on test preparation, and good student scores on standardized tests.

Okay, now consider these questions: Yes, in your school the hallways are carefully supervised and quiet. Does that mean students are learning in the classrooms? The attendance rate in your school is good. Does that mean that students are learning when they are at school? Your school offers many AP or Baccalaureate classes. Does that mean that all students are learning in their classes? Your school graduates most of its students. Does that mean that students are learning in their classes? Your school really gets very focused on preparing for the state test. Does that mean students are learning? Your school does well on state and federal tests. Does that mean students are really learning?

Of course, because of your honest perspective, you know that none of these evaluation points really guarantees that students are learning. What's worse is that for each of these marking points, teachers and school leaders have a way of fudging the data so things look better than they really are.

Certainly you know that many students graduate that have learned very little. And you know that many students who attend school are really "in-school dropouts" who do almost nothing when they are in school. And you have probably heard that many AP or Baccalaureate classes are filled with students who don't want to be there and can't do the work and that many such students just game that class just like any other class.

Finally, you have probably faced in yourself that even though your students did well on the Big State Test, they would never think of it as an important learning experience. While the adults spend lots of time focusing on these points, they neglect opportunities to encourage real learning. How? By sharing perspectives, having a conversation with students—a conversation about what is really going on in school—and how students might be invited to make a personal investment in learning and learn in an authentic way.

So just like students, teachers and school leaders have ways of making the data show what they want it to show so they keep their superiors happy. Like students, they create the appearance of compliance because that is really what gets evaluated, not genuine student learning. One way they do this is by teaching to the test. That means instead of letting student learning go in many possible directions, all learning is focused on the standardized test. It is a method teachers use to keep up appearances.

Regretfully, some teachers and administrators have even resorted to cheating. As this book is being written, teachers in a number of cities in the United States are being prosecuted for changing student answers and falsifying their schools' test results. These teachers and administrators were creating false appearances; they were playing the game of school.

So what does all of this mean for you as a teacher of prospective teachers? Hopefully, it means you are helping your students face the reality of these conditions and getting them to talk frankly about them. They are, after all, students, and they know what is really going on in their school. Getting your students to talk frankly about the game of school is the first step in stopping it.

But is there a way of stopping the game of school and getting kids authentically involved in trying to learn and prepare for their futures? As you think about this question, remember these three things:

1. If your school leaders are not checking on student engagement by asking them questions about how they experience school, then the school leaders really don't know if students are learning in a deep way.
2. Everybody knows that just because a student is getting good grades does not mean that the student is learning. Lots of students at school who are getting excellent grades have made no personal investment in their learning. Their learning is not deep. They are just learning strategically, doing what they have to do to get the grades they want.
3. The reason most states give big tests at the end of the year to check student learning is because they don't trust the grades that teachers give students. They know those grades are often inflated, like a lot of the other data that comes out of schools.

That last item is a rough one. The state doesn't trust how teachers evaluate students. How do you feel about that? Why the state doesn't trust teacher evaluations has to do with the game of school. Can you see the connection? Can you see this situation as a reason to get your students to assert teacher leadership toward more honorable and authentic learning?

EVEN GOVERNMENT OFFICIALS PLAY THE GAME OF SCHOOL

An even more difficult fact to face is that the important people in your town, your county, your state, and the nation also play the game of school. These people are called the policymakers. They tell the schools what they have to do. And they play the game just like the students because they focus on how they are going to be judged, not on real student learning.

Remember, the game of school is about creating the appearance of doing what you are supposed to do. So the policymakers come up with a strategy to make it look as if they are dealing with the problem of low-quality learning in schools. Thus, they direct the schools to improve learning. They do this with fanfare and news headlines. In addition, they require students to take standardized tests. These tests are intended to show the public that the state is getting tough on the schools. Then policymakers put tremendous pressure on the school leaders to come up with better test scores. They threaten to fire principals and to withhold money from the schools if scores do not improve.

School leaders then do everything they can to get high test scores even though focusing on the test scores means they stop paying attention to other things that students should learn. Nevertheless, all of this creates the right appearance that policymakers are actively trying to improve schools by raising standards. God knows we have all heard a lot about raising standards over the last thirty years.

But did student learning improve? As it turns out, in spite of all of the effort and money spent over the course of decades, the report card is not so good. As previously cited, the report on the long-term trends in student reading and math achievement based on NAEP scores reads, "Average reading and math scores in 2012 for 17-year-olds were not significantly different from scores in the first assessment year" (IES, 2012).

That first year was 1971. So after all of the years of standardized testing and all of the headlines about getting tough with schools and raising standards, the government's own report card indicates student learning has not improved over the last forty years. Yet with the coming of each new president, the media was flush with headlines that gave the appearance that leaders were doing what they were supposed to do.

It's just like when the students in school focus on getting good grades instead of learning and getting personally invested in learning. Like your local school leaders, policymakers don't ask the students about how they experience secondary school or listen to their opinions about whether or not they think they are really learning. Instead of focusing on deep understanding of the schooling process, they opt to create appearances with legislation and headlines and then keep it simple, a single test score.

There are Two Kinds of Learning

One: Authentic Learning

> Authentic learning is when you do it because you like doing it, because you enjoy the challenge, you enjoy the process, you want to do more of it, and you like the confidence you get when you have acquired new knowledge and skills. When you experience authentic learning, it makes you feel like you have been changed and you want more of it.

Two: Superficial Strategic Learning

> The superficial learning we usually do in secondary school is different. This is not learning you do out of enjoyment of the subject or the challenge. You do it to get the grades or awards you need to keep your parents and teachers happy and to look good to your friends. You do it because you have to, and you want to get it over with.
>
> Then what? You forget all the things you memorized for the class and weeks later you can hardly remember anything. Then you realize, "Gosh, I hardly learned anything in that class." Even worse, students start to get this bad feeling about school and learning. They start to avoid it. They just want to get it over with. This happens over and over again to students in secondary school. You hear secondary school students say it all of the time. They call it a "joke." But it is **NOT** funny.

Figure 10.1.

REAL RIGOR MATTERS

One of the primary problems with the gaming culture that develops in secondary schools is that it interferes with genuine rigor. Nowadays it is popular for education leaders to talk about rigor. Rigor is when a person gets deeply involved with and works really hard to get something right or achieve deep understanding.

These education leaders are right. Experiencing rigor *is* an important part of getting ready for college and a lifetime of learning. One of the reasons experiencing rigor is important is because rigor leads to success. But an often overlooked aspect of rigor is that it is an experience of fulfillment. It is a time when an individual can see and experience the relationship between effort, personal growth, personal identity, happiness, and getting things done. Genuine rigor feels good. It does not feel like slavery or servitude.

Authentic rigor is when an individual is so determined and engaged in what they are doing that they work really hard at it because it feels good; it feels right. Sometimes it feels almost effortless, and people are often reluctant to stop or slow down when they undertake such work. When you engage in rigor, it is more often than not because you really like what you are working on and you have some personal commitment to it.

Unfortunately, disciplined compliance is often mistaken for rigor. Disciplined compliance is when a student knows what must be achieved to get the desired grade. So, the student works extremely hard to do something exceptional in order to get the grade or award. But this student does not identify with the work. She does not enjoy the challenge or the discovery. The work has no meaning except to get the reward.

As a teacher of prospective teachers, it is important to clarify for students that as they operate now, schools actually encourage students to think strategically and to seek high grades without deeply appreciating the experience or value of the learning process. It tells them that it is the score that matters, not the experience of rigor and learning.

THERE IS A SOLUTION TO THE GAME OF SCHOOL

Stopping the game of school begins with facing it and talking about it. That means that young people and adults must admit that it is going on. They must put their cards on the table and talk about it with each other. Schools should encourage students to talk about the gaming of school and show them how it contrasts with the real learning engagement. Such discussions could encourage all stakeholders to try new approaches and drive the evolution of teaching and learning.

Ask yourself this: Have you ever led or participated in a discussion in your school about the game of school? Have you ever led or participated in a discussion that distinguished between strategic learning and authentic learning? Now that you have some ideas about these phenomena, do you also have a sense of how students might learn more authentically?

At the end of this chapter, there is another textbox, Public School Teachers Are Leading the Way. In this case it was the author's work, a career high school teacher. During his previously cited research, he asked students what they thought would help get them away from gaming school. Their observations have been distilled into these ten points cited by students in chapter 5 of his research report (Waters, 2012).

In addition to this textbox, readers are referred to the upcoming contrast drawn between a twentieth-century school and a twenty-first-century school in chapter 12. Your review of these observations should point you to a very different kind of learning environment than the one in a traditional school. A twenty-first-century school environment encourages authentic learning, not gaming.

AGAIN, IT IS ABOUT SHARING PERSPECTIVES

Many educators, however, do not want to discuss the game of school or students' real levels of engagement because that would be the beginning of revealing the shallowness in much of the school experience. Ask yourself, right now, in your school is there any recognition of the game of school? Does anyone talk about the difference between strategic learning and authentic learning?

These questions bring us back to the importance of students and teachers sharing perspectives. The game of school is a very real thing that is often observed in research. Yet no one talks about it. How can we end the game of school, if people are not talking about it and sharing perspectives on how we might make learning more real? This again is an opportunity for leadership for our future teachers.

But again, this book is about helping you help aspiring teachers think about what it will mean to be a teacher. The fact is that this book wants to encourage your students to become teachers. Hopefully, they will be teachers who are willing to face the realities and challenges explained here, and they will see that learning needs to be approached in some new ways and that schools do need to make some changes.

CONCLUSION

This chapter has been about something that everybody knows about and nobody wants to talk about, the game of school. The game of school is about people pretending to do what they are supposed to do at school. Students, teachers, and policymakers all play the game of school. The game of school encourages shallow, strategic learning just to get grades, awards, promotion, and college acceptance.

As teachers of future generations, what will your students do to stop the game of school?

DISCUSSION QUESTIONS

1. Explain how the game of school plays a role in your school.

2. Explain how the game of school hurts real learning.
3. Why would it be a good idea to get everybody in your school talking about the game of school?

LEADERSHIP ACTIVITIES

1. Survey students about how they play the game of school.
2. Find out which students would be willing to participate in a public discussion about the game of school and the harm it does.

TEXTBOX 10.1. PUBLIC SCHOOL TEACHERS ARE LEADING THE WAY

Stopping the Game of School

Recent research at an East Coast high school brought together students in a Tomorrow's Teachers class to discuss the game of school and how to stop it. The researcher asked students what conditions would be necessary to get away from the game of school and low-value education in "learning to look good" and to move schools toward personally meaningful learning for all students.

Students' answers were used in developing the following list, called The Learning Value Zone. Look at the list below. Do your students agree with this list? Can they think of some other experience they might add to it?

THE LEARNING VALUE ZONE

1. I feel that the teachers and students around me really care about me and my progress.
2. I know that my individual differences and uniqueness as a learner are appreciated.
3. I know my teachers and school leaders have an interest in how I experience school.
4. I see my personal strengths, weaknesses, talents, and goals are being clarified.
5. I'm discovering my intrinsic motives for learning.
6. I enjoy the work I do at school, and I'm discovering the pleasures of learning.

7. I sense that my school work is relevant and has purpose now and for my future.
8. I sense my personal growth in knowledge, skills, and social maturity.
9. I influence and make choices regarding what and how I learn.
10. I feel very optimistic and excited about my future. (Waters, 2012)

Most of your students have probably never thought about the value of what they get at school in these terms. But because they are thinking about being teachers, they should. Yes, they know when they have a great teacher or a poor one, but they have probably never broken it down like this.

If they were to use this list to evaluate their experience at school, how much value do they think they are getting? If you were to use this list to evaluate your work as a teacher, how much value would you be giving? Do you see that how we think of learning in schools needs to evolve, how it needs to get to a place where students actually want to do the work?

Your students need to be prepared for this: as our concept of learning evolves in the future, everyone will pay more attention to how students experience learning. They won't just look at test scores. Now is an especially good time to get your students to recognize how often they feel the value at school. They need to start thinking about how often their learning is high quality and personally important and when it is the cheap stuff they did just to get the grades they want. Teachers making this distinction will be an important benchmark in the evolution of teaching and learning.

III

Teachers Leading the Evolution of Teaching and Learning

Chapter Eleven

The Story of Jane

This chapter is based on one big example. It is about a fictitious girl named Jane, but, again, Jane's story has been inspired by research. Jane loved to dance, and this story is about how she came to take ownership of her education while working with a learning coach.

As they read Jane's story, each of your students should be asked to think about how a similar story would unfold if (1) this story were about one of their students and how she was helped to pursue an area of interest that she really wanted to learn; (2) if she were a teacher guiding a student's learning.

When Jane and her coach started working together, Jane explained that she recalled a longstanding love of dance in her childhood, and that her parents often encouraged her in dancing as a child. When she got older, though, school became more demanding, and there seemed fewer and fewer opportunities for dancing.

Jane enjoyed going to teen parties for dancing, but it wasn't enough for her. Then she remembered going through a long period where she nearly forgot about her love of dancing. Eventually, in the ninth grade she went out for a small dancing part in a musical at her secondary school. She enjoyed the experience, and it brought back to her how much she loved dancing. She decided that she had to do more to follow this personal passion.

Working with her learning coach, Jane mapped out a personal learning plan for herself. Right from the start, it was explained to Jane that everything she chose to put in her personal learning plan had to be fun and exciting. Otherwise, her learning coach wouldn't agree to it.

At first Jane didn't seem to get it. She would say to her learning coach, "Wow, it doesn't seem possible that I'm going to design a learning plan that won't be boring at least some of the time like a lot of the stuff at school." It was as if Jane didn't believe that learning could be that much fun. Let's see what she came up with.

The first thing Jane and her learning coach tried to do was bring some happy learning into Jane's evening hours when her homework was done. Of course, one of the first things was to get some books that Jane might *want* to read. She didn't have to read them, but she decided she would go to the library and pick out several that she thought she might like.

As part of this effort, she went to her musical theater teacher and asked if she had any recommendations. Her teacher suggested Twyla Tharp's *The Creative Habit* and Eric Franklin's *Dance Imagery*. Then she and her learning coach decided to check out a few films, which included *The Turning Point, Singin' in the Rain*, and *Shall We Dance* that were about the lives of dancers or featured great dancing.

One afternoon a couple of weeks later, Jane and her parents met with the learning coach. She told the learning coach that she was really getting into her books, and she was starting to get an idea that would be really fun and exciting. She wanted to take the bus into New York City (from New Jersey) to go to a professional dance presentation. Of course, her learning coach thought it was a great idea but suggested that she take a while to decide what she wanted to see.

Jane's learning coach gave her several copies of the *New York Times* so she could look through the arts section, check out the ads, and read some dance reviews. She shared these with her mother and father, and they selected a dance recital at New York University as their first venture. Jane also took a friend from school.

Within a matter of months Jane had created a learning program for herself that was full of dance. This included registering and networking at several dance websites and assisting at a local dance studio working with small children in exchange for dance lessons and a place to work out. Jane's learning coach was terrifically pleased with her progress, but the next big step was to bring Jane's personal learning plan into the school, the place where she was supposed to be getting her education.

Jane was apprehensive about this, but after a lengthy discussion with her learning coach and parents, she decided to start small and work her way up. Jane's secondary school only offered two dance classes, but signing up for the advanced class was her first big effort.

Next, Jane and her learning coach looked at all of her classes and tried to figure out whether or not she could take advantage of some choice assignments such as research papers, book reports, personal essays, and even projects in biology. As it turned out, there were some possibilities. Jane wrote a history research paper on the development of modern dance and its relationship to the development of jazz in the United States.

Eventually, Jane did several book reports on books about dance and dance personalities. She also wrote a personal essay on her decision to get serious about really pursuing her life's passion, and she completed a biology project on anatomical considerations in dancing. She even studied several famous dance paintings for a project in her art class and took a stab at a pen-and-ink self-portrait based on a photo of her dancing.

Jane and her learning coach were really happy about her successes in getting her class assignments to accommodate her personal passion. But what Jane did next really had visible impact on her school. She started to get a grand plan in mind. The first thing she did was to go to her dance teacher and propose to be her apprentice and to actually make her apprenticeship a class for credit during the upcoming semester.

Jane explained to her teacher that she was deeply invested in dance in a very personal way and that she really believed she could help her teacher prepare the ninth-graders. The idea of a student being a teacher's apprentice had never been considered before at her school, but amazingly, Jane's teacher was moved by her initiative and agreed to do the groundwork that would allow her to be her apprentice in her senior year as a for-credit, independent study program.

The next thing Jane did was to start a dance club so students interested in dance could get together to exchange ideas and experiences and to do some exploring in how to bring even more dance into their lives. The club drew on a broad range of students, male and female, including a group of young men who were into break dancing. In addition to some great socializing, the club became a venue for exchanging books, watching movies together, guest speakers, recitals, and club trips to a variety of dance presentations, which attracted more and more students to the club.

One last note about Jane involves her final semester senior project, which was not about dance. Jane experienced so much success in secondary school because she found ways to bring her personal passion into her work that she took the initiative to make another change at her school. She asked permission to mentor five incoming ninth-graders in the second term of their freshman year. As their mentor, she made a big effort to help these students get in touch with their personal interests, passions, missions, and callings so they could begin to learn in an intentional way, a way that was as fun and exciting as Jane's had been.

The fact is that this was not an easy project for her, and she admitted at the end that she probably should have mentored just one student. She quickly discovered that all of the students were confused by the idea that they would be allowed to pursue topics that they found fun and exciting.

Nevertheless, all of the students eventually did begin to make the transition and start to figure out ways to bring their personal passions—turtles, back packing, motorcycles, beach photography, and amusement parks—into their work at school. Each student started to discover that when they pursued their passion, they also learned vocabulary, reading, science, math, literature, art, history, and more.

THE MEANING OF PERSONAL PASSIONS

Very often when the story of Jane is shared, people question, "What if Jane made the wrong choice in secondary school, and her real passion was something else?" It's a great question. It provides a chance to explain something very important. When a young person decides to actively influence her education, the important thing is not about what she thinks that passion is (because they do change). The important thing is the experience of making a decision and taking ownership of one's learning.

Taking ownership of your learning is about learning to stand up and take charge. That's where the real learning is. It's about making that connection between being in charge of your learning and having a personal purpose and how that leads to much deeper learning. A real education is not about being a passive doer; it involves a lot of reflection, decision making, learning how to learn, and taking action. It is about developing the habit of looking deeply into yourself, of reflecting on who you are, and making your own decisions about what you need to do in order to move forward.

This story raises many questions for aspiring teachers. Primary is this idea of learning ownership. This is not a concept that comes up a lot in a traditional school. In a traditional school, successful students do what they are assigned. They don't usually have a strong sense of ownership over their assignments because it wasn't their idea to do the work in the first place. They were just doing what was required of them.

Then the question arises, Should teachers want students to take ownership of their learning? Should teachers encourage students to ask themselves the following questions about the schoolwork they do?

> Why am I doing this?
> Do I feel my heart is really in it?
> Could I do it in a different way that would bring my heart into it?
> Am I directing my own learning, or am I being a robot and allowing others to direct me?
> How will letting others make these important decisions for me affect my ability to make good decisions for myself in the future?

CONCLUSION

This chapter is an illustration of how a student was prompted to take ownership of her learning. As you read Jane's story, you probably thought about how such a story would develop if it were about you. The truth is that at school most students don't take ownership of their learning. But it is also true that it is not part of traditional teaching to offer that ownership to students.

The guiding question here is this: Are your students going to be teachers who understand the benefits of offering ownership of learning to their students?

DISCUSSION QUESTIONS

1. Did Jane's story give you a few ideas about how to take control of your own learning? What are they?
2. Does Jane's story give you some ideas about how teaching might change in the future? Please share these ideas.

LEADERSHIP ACTIVITIES

1. Write down some ideas about how you could change what you do in your classes so it relates to topics you really care about.
2. Talk with your teachers about the possibility of the school allowing prospective teachers to become apprentices to teachers while they are still in secondary school.

Chapter Twelve

Let's Imagine a Twenty-First-Century Secondary School

The introduction of this book explained that it was going to help you help your students think about the meaning of being a teacher. Part of that process has been to get them to imagine themselves in some new roles as teachers. Of course, many of those new roles will emerge from the fact that they have embraced the idea of students and teachers sharing perspectives for school improvement. This chapter will focus on providing prompts to help your students imagine some of those new roles.

In all of the information presented here, your students will again be faced with choosing the structures and practices of a traditional teacher in a traditional school or possibly influencing their learning communities to undertake new structures and new practices that they believe will facilitate more authentic learning for students and teachers.

Along the way, they may start to get some of their own ideas for new approaches to learning that you know as a teacher would address problems you see in your own experience in a traditional school. When this happens they will be fulfilling the purpose of this book.

The idea here is not to insist that new schools will be any one way. Rather, in the future, a new breed of teachers will be constantly creating new kinds of schools and always experimenting with new approaches to teaching and learning. This will be the outcome of doing what authentic learning communities do:

1. Persist in a lively sharing of perspectives about learning, instruction, and schooling.
2. Design their own learning experiences to answer their own questions about the conditions of schooling and things they need to know to

improve the school. Such learning may involve book research, examination of their personal experiences, using technology, conducting surveys, working in the broader community, doing interviews, and more.
3. Form goals and develop action plans.
4. Take collective action to achieve their goals to improve their learning community, their school, or their broader community.

In this way, schools will not all be the same, and schools will no longer be stuck with the same structure and practices for the next one hundred years.

FOCUS ON THE STUDENT, NOT THE BUILDING

For now, your students probably need more concrete clarity about how twenty-first-century schools would be different and why they would be better. This chapter is going to try to provide you and your students with examples from a secondary school, the situation they are in now. Much of what you and they will see will be an outcome of insights and information from the preceding chapters.

To begin with, when most people think about a secondary school, they often think about a secondary school building. It's usually a large, expansive building with long hallways lined with classrooms and student lockers. Twentieth-century secondary schools make most of what students do in secondary school conform to the secondary school building.

Twenty-first-century secondary schools will probably focus less on the building and more on customized learning programs and personal service to students wherever and however that might work best for them. Upcoming examples will show that much more of the learning in a twenty-first-century school will happen outside of the school building and involve community partners who stand to contribute a great deal to student learning.

Earlier, the reader was asked to consider two approaches to learning: strategic learning and authentic learning. Right now we know that most secondary schools today produce the type of student who does schoolwork in order to look good. These are the students who do what they have to do to get good grades in order to please their parents, teachers, and peers even though they are not getting personally involved in and enjoying their learning.

By contrast, the objective of a twenty-first-century secondary school would be to create students who want authentic learning. These are the students who learn because they really want to. (It's hard to believe that such students really exist, but research has shown that they do exist (Childress, 2000; Cushman, 2010; Damon, 2008; Waters, 2012). You will get a better understanding as you keep reading. These students enjoy what they do because they are studying and doing things that they really want to know about; they decide what it is that they want to study; and they have an idea about how it will help them become the person they want to be.

When we consider how these two hypothetical students are different, we start to get an idea of how a twenty-first-century secondary school will be different and how it would be better. A twenty-first-century secondary school will focus on getting students deeply engaged by offering them highly individualized and customized learning that appeals to their personal strengths, talents, interests, and ambitions.

UNIQUE COMMUNITIES NEED UNIQUE SCHOOLS

One of the things we know for sure about secondary schools of the twenty-first century is that they will not all be the same (Kelly et al., 2009). In the future, every community will constantly be creating and recreating their school(s) based on the needs and aspirations of all of the stakeholders (students, parents, teachers, school, and community leaders). Many communities will likely have more than one secondary school (possibly several small schools) because stakeholders with different needs and aspirations may want to have their own unique school.

The wonderful thing is that everybody will be constantly thinking about learning and what a school can do to improve how it helps students. It won't be like it is today where secondary schools continue to do what they have always done for the last one hundred years and more. And in twenty-first-century secondary schools students as members of the learning community will be sharing perspectives and informing the adults about what is working and what is not, and students will expect the adults to stop doing things that don't work and to try new strategies to help students learn.

Right now some readers may still be thinking that a secondary school that is highly individualized would be unrealistic. These readers probably think that no school could set up a program of study for each student that is customized to the needs and desires of each individual. Some readers are also probably thinking that some students might just pick easy classes where they have to do very little.

Having these thoughts is understandable, but it also means that such thinking may be suffering from school blindness. This is also understandable because the only secondary school most people have ever known has been a twentieth-century secondary school. So it is hard to imagine that a school that is very, very different is really possible. But as has already been said, such schools already exist.

TWENTY-FIRST-CENTURY SECONDARY SCHOOL STUDENT SCHEDULE

So the point of this chapter is to help you imagine a twenty-first-century secondary school and the new roles it would offer teachers; that is, imagine a secondary school that would create students who really want to learn, not just go through the motions pretending to learn. So to help you do some imagining about a twenty-first-century secondary school, here is an example of a twenty-first-century student's secondary school schedule.

8:30 a.m.: Home: Check into online course in Japanese and Skype with Japanese students who are home completing homework assignments for an English class at their school in Japan.

10:30 a.m.: City Hall (Basement): Meet with City Service Project Group on Pure Water Sustainability. There is a discussion of two articles projecting worldwide water shortages. A water utility employee teaches the seminar. She is referred to as a Community Partner Teacher.

12:00 p.m.: 140 Main Street: Working lunch at secondary school satellite meeting room in downtown office building with teacher and project crew to explore a downtown park and pond as an ecosystem. The teacher is a county employee and is also a Community Partner Teacher from the County Task Force on Environmental Care. She lives in the community and has created and volunteered to teach this course.

1:30 p.m.: Secondary School, Room 308: Poetry Class: Hip Hop/Slam/Tumble/Break Out. This class was created and marketed by a traditional English teacher on staff at the old secondary school before change started. To increase staff and student ownership of teaching and learning, he and other teachers have started to invent and market their own classes in cooperation with students. If students don't sign up for the classes, they are no longer offered.

2:30 p.m.: Secondary School Writing Center: Group critique of dialogue being developed for a documentary film about the senior prom.

3:15 p.m.: America's Field: Track practice with team. Along with the secondary school coach, a man and woman from the community who have deep backgrounds in track are assisting students.

5:30 p.m.: Home: Dinner with family.

6:30 p.m.: Home: Film crew and Community Partner film teacher meet in home basement to plan film locations. This teacher is also a community resident whose profession involves doing short films and commercials for ad agencies. Students recruited him to help with this film project. It has become customary for students to invent their own courses and recruit teachers from inside the faculty or from the regional community.

8:30 p.m.: Home: Check into online course: Culture, Politics, and DNA. This course is provided by a corporation that provides online courses to school districts around the world. This student found the course relevant to his interest in how local community decisions contribute to better use of natural resources.

Independent Reading: *Harry Potter and* . . .

Saturday Elective: Six-hour, communication competency workshop: The Role of Males in a More Feminine World.

Note: All of the courses cited above were one-semester courses (eighteen weeks). This student also completed some short-term courses that were offered on weekends, evenings, and during the summer. This included a Workshop, "Quadratic Equations and Video Games" (three hours on both Friday night and Saturday night and the writing of a combined personal essay/equation demonstration), and "Athletes as Community Leaders," which met on Monday night for five weeks and required initiating and writing about a small but helpful community project.

Over the summer, this student developed competencies and received credit for completing and keeping records on a running training routine, taking three online math courses (over three summers) and writing a short play based on his discovery that a close friend and teammate was gay. In the final year of secondary school, this student completed a course, Personal Essay, with a private tutor with whom he met once a week. This student would complete secondary school in three years.

Also note that in this community, secondary school courses were offered on their home sites by the police department (two courses), the fire department (two courses), the local hospital (three courses), the city manager's office (one course), the mayor's office (one course), the Office of Animal Control (two courses), and the Chamber of Commerce (two courses).

In addition, courses were offered by professionals who lived in the community and came to students' homes to teach courses in law, veterinary medicine, stocks and bonds, antiques, child guidance, government, local history, local geology, beach ecology, microbiology, professional music recording, gardening, small business start-up, writing professionally, ballooning, kite art, home construction, cabinet making, and Victorian home restoration.

DATA ANALYTICS

This student's career path and higher education choices were informed by data analytics. What this means is that this student would be helped to avoid making bad career and higher-education choices based on what's popular, prestigious, or what looks beautiful in a college catalogue. Instead, this student would be helped to choose a career and higher education based on being a "good fit" with the student's actual personality, financial resources, values, and goals.

How does this work? Think of it this way. Throughout a student's schooling, elementary and secondary, a lot of data is collected from this student. This data might include a record of a student's in and out of school behavior, in and out of school choices, as well as performance around school, in classrooms, and online. Eventually, this accumulated data provides students with objective feedback on where their passions lie, what their strengths are, where they need help, and which higher-education options will likely be best suited to the individual student's advancement.

The collection and interpretation of such data is assisted by an ever-growing array of data analytic commercial products such as Knewton, Learning Catalytics, myEDMatch.com, Naviance, ConnectEDU, eAdvisor, or Degree Compass. Such analytic programs help students avoid bad choices and can improve a student's reflection on what careers and higher education choices fit the student's personality, why they are a better fit, as well as indicate specific careers, training schools, colleges, and universities that would be a good fit for the student.

WHAT WOULD YOUR STUDENTS' SCHEDULES LOOK LIKE?

Now it is your students' turn. Just for fun, ask them to take a minute by themselves or with some friends to create their own fantasy schedules. And remember, the point of this chapter is to help them *imagine* a new kind of secondary school, one where they would have real interest in what they studied. Or, as teachers, they could invent their own courses that would get students involved in authentic learning.

So they would need to think about what they would really want to learn or teach and how that learning could be fun and exciting. Your students should be encouraged to write anything down that they want, even if it is weird (weird is good). *There is one rule: their schedules must be fun and exciting.* To assist their imaginations, below is a list of twenty-first-century learning activities. They may want to use some of these in their own way.

TWENTY-FIRST-CENTURY LEARNING ACTIVITIES

Consider These Projects

Documentaries
Podcasts
Websites

Global communication
Email exchanges: a history, a play, a short story, a painting (Yes, a painting!)
Digital music compositions
Webcasts from live sites
Films
Online courses
Teaching machines and software
Video podcasts
Screenplays
Quarterly e-reports
Video conferences
Simulations
Simulation games
Second Life simulations, visitations, participations
Travel writing
Unbelievable independent projects with technology
Video teaching
Video games
Serious board games
Global contacts social networking

CONSIDER THESE SCHOOL-BASED LEARNING ACTIVITIES

1. Advisories
2. Collaborative projects
3. Global collaborative projects
4. Independent study projects
5. Online courses
6. Student-invented off-site courses with satellite teachers
7. Distance classes provided at home, a community location, or at the secondary school
8. Instructional video games
9. Apprenticeships with teacher or community mentors
10. Community service projects
11. Performances or exhibitions
12. Teaching other students
13. Extended observations of a professional at work
14. Completing a course of programmed study
15. Completing open coursework with an online provider
16. Completing a travel project
17. Maintaining a blog

18. Starting a business and studying it
19. Taking a job and studying it
20. Building a prototype or a historical replica
21. Conducting a survey, completing statistical work, writing conclusions
22. Doing action research in school or the community; contributing to solving the problem, writing about it
23. Guiding others in action research
24. Writing a play, screenplay, short story, novella, or novel
25. Creating your own class, finding your own teacher, writing the curriculum with goals and objectives, and taking the class
26. Tutoring a student in a foreign country in English
27. Mentoring a younger student
28. Studying yourself: on a diet, in a play, playing a sport, breaking up with your boyfriend or girlfriend, preparing for a date, going to the prom, on an adventure, helping a friend, giving a gift
29. Taking a college course
30. Taking a video course
31. Learning about and creating an electronic portfolio
32. Studying meaningful involvement in school operations
33. Taking a class in independent/collaborative study and project design
34. Turning a club into a class
35. Doing a study on the school
36. Producing a TV program
37. Publishing a magazine
38. Writing a history of your family, street, pets, or anything that is meaningful for you

QUESTIONS FOR STUDENTS

If You Actually Did Complete a Fantasy Schedule:

1. Did you make it fun and exciting?
2. Does it show that you want to put a lot of energy into learning and growing a wonderful life?
3. Do you think the things you would learn from your fantasy schedule would be meaningful and help you develop into the adult that you want to become?
4. Do you see that your subject choices would also help you advance in traditional subjects like reading, writing, calculation, speaking, and critical thinking?

5. Do you think that if you were actually allowed to have such a schedule that you would spend a lot of time disconnecting, gaming school, and just pretending to be a student?

At some point, your students might be thinking that, yes, my fantasy schedule is very nice, and I think I would learn a lot, but I still don't think it is a possibility. Their concern is understandable, but consider this: right now there are some adults (not teachers) who are thinking about how to change secondary schools. Would your students like the adults who are planning new kinds of schools to consider the opinions of students, especially prospective teachers? Do they think the ideas and feelings of students and teachers should be part of the change process?

A fundamental idea in this book is that it is *absolutely necessary* to have teachers and students participate in the planning. Think about it. Secondary schools are all about getting students ready for adult life. If the planners don't hear their ideas and feelings about how well secondary schools are working, how will they know if what they plan is really helping them? The student point of view counts! Your and their leadership will be crucial.

As they consider the choices in front of them, they should also consider the upcoming two descriptions. The following lists describe how two different kinds of schools function. The lists are based on research that tells us that students will respond to learning opportunities based on how the teachers and schools present the opportunities to learn (Ames & Archer, 1988; Blackwell et al., 2007; Deci et al., 1991; Dweck & Leggett, 1988; Grant & Dweck, 2003; Mueller & Dweck, 1998; Reeve, 2002; Ryan & Deci, 2000).

Your students already know that schools and teachers can influence how students think of learning. They probably have some ideas of their own about how to improve that influence. What the list suggests is that some teacher strategies can result in students just learning to please the people around them. Other strategies can result in students getting personally invested in learning and giving it a great effort.

LEARNING CULTURE IN A TWENTY-FIRST-CENTURY SECONDARY SCHOOL

Focus on Individualization, Personalization, and Customization of Learning

1. Teachers present and discuss lots of learning choices for the students.
2. The school provides many electives and encourages student-initiated courses and anytime, anywhere learning opportunities.

3. Teachers always recognize and emphasize effort (hours devoted, start-overs, extraordinary behavior) as key to learning.
4. Teachers recognize commitment (the mindset that a person loves or finds special meaning in certain activities or work).
5. Technology is used to individualize, personalize, and customize learning.
6. Teachers recognize that effort is a searching mechanism (it always leads to a new frontier, new efforts, and a personal step forward in understanding the self and the world).
7. Students help teachers reflect on their teaching techniques and instructional practices.
8. Teachers provide demonstrations of and invitations to complete complicated, long-term projects and problem solving.
9. Teachers listen to and respond to students' concerns about boring experiences. And teachers explain why some boring experiences or work are necessary if they are.
10. Students are provided opportunities to demonstrate knowledge of nuanced information or skills.
11. Students are provided opportunities to employ and/or demonstrate personal strengths.
12. Students are provided opportunities to help other students improve.
13. Students are provided opportunities for fun, flow, and zoning in subjects of passion.
14. Students are provided opportunities to express intrinsic motivation.
15. Students are provided opportunities to network and work in groups.
16. Students are frequently invited to be creative.
17. There is adult acceptance of mistakes, setbacks, and dead ends.
18. There is regular reflection on efforts, goals, and achievements, putting it in the whole-life context.
19. There is regular reflection on students' emerging sense of purpose in life.
20. There are one or two teachers who know a student in a deep way and provide guidance.
21. When teachers collaborate on critical lessons, they are primarily focused on making the lesson engaging, novel, fun, exciting, and adventurous.
22. Assessment is provided that includes models, benchmarks, and student participation.
23. Assessment is based primarily on demonstrations and artifacts (performances, presentation, demonstrations, portfolios, and e-portfolios).

LEARNING CULTURE IN A TWENTY-FIRST-CENTURY SECONDARY SCHOOL

Focus on Standardization of Knowledge, Skills, and Assessment

1. Teachers and school leaders frequently talk about important requirements, government mandates, testing, and fixed schedules.
2. Teachers and school leaders emphasize that most learning challenges are requirements and the school offers few electives. Electives are thought of as less important "fun and games" classes.
3. Teachers and school leaders focus on evaluation outcomes (letter grades or other scaling devices, test scores) over effort or process.
4. Teachers and school leaders give lots of recognition for compliance. Students are appreciated for working hard even when the work is not interesting or meaningful.
5. Technology is used to standardize what students learn, how they learn it, and how they will be evaluated.
6. Teachers and school leaders promote decontextualized learning (students are expected to do work because "it is good for you" without understanding its place in their lives or the world).
7. Teachers and school leaders do not seek student input on how to improve teaching and learning.
8. Teachers and school leaders emphasize memorization, right answers, work completion, and short answer or multiple choice testing.
9. Students experience schoolwork as routines of compliance (just getting the work done with little personal interest so you don't get in trouble).
10. Teachers are not interested in student complaints about being bored in school. They give stock responses about the student needing the knowledge and needing to take an interest in their education.
11. Students are almost always listening, never presenting their expertise.
12. Students' personal strengths are unrecognized in favor of learning requirements.
13. There are no formal opportunities for students to employ their strengths to help others.
14. Teachers and school leaders place emphasis on extrinsic motivation: learn in order to get good grades, keep parents happy, get respect of peers, get into a good college, get a good job, make good money.
15. Teachers and school leaders offer few or no opportunities for students to express intrinsic motivation (doing things you want to do just because you enjoy doing them).
16. Students sit alone in single desks and do work primarily by themselves.

17. Work assignments require following routines and formulas, not creativity.
18. Mistakes and setbacks result in lower grades.
19. Coursework involves little or no reflection on efforts, goals, and achievement; no putting it in the whole-life context.
20. There is no reflection on students' emerging sense of purpose in life.
21. Students have no dedicated individual relationship with one or more adults at school.
22. When teachers prepare lessons, they are primarily focused on exposing students to information or skills as required in the curriculum or state standards.
23. Teachers use assessment tools that do not include models, benchmarks, or student input on design.
24. Assessment is primarily based on short-answer testing and quizzes, compliance assignments such as homework completion and book reports, and unchallenging projects such as drawing a map or baking a cake (no portfolios or e-portfolios).

When your students consider both of these descriptive lists, they should get a sense of the clear choice they have in selecting the kind of teachers they want to be. Right now, if they were to go to Google and search the topic "twenty-first-century secondary schools," they would see that there are people and groups focused on the idea of changing secondary schools. The question is this: Would they as secondary school students and prospective teachers like to be part of that conversation about how to change schools?

CONCLUSION

This chapter tried to help readers imagine new roles for students and teachers in schools of the future. These schools of the future will not all be the same, and students and teachers working together with local stakeholders to meet the needs of local students will create them. If you and your students like the idea of students and teachers working together to create new kinds of schools, that is where your students' leadership is crucial. Without leadership that has a new vision of how learning can happen, the most important members of schools, students and teachers, might be left out.

What will that leadership look like? The next chapter will help with that question.

DISCUSSION QUESTIONS

1. How does the idea of schools becoming very different from what you have experienced make you feel?
2. How do you feel about the idea of you becoming a leader of change?

LEADERSHIP ACTIVITY

Survey the teachers in your school to see what they think about some of the big changes suggested in this book.

The Action Manual

Your Leadership Now Leads to Your Leadership Later

Now you and your students have considered the ideas in this book. They have had an opportunity to think about some of the big-picture, strategic questions regarding the meaning of being a teacher. They have had an opportunity to think about what it means for teachers to be thinkers, decision makers, and leaders. Now the question becomes, What do *they* do about it? What can any secondary school student do about anything?

To answer this question, this Action Manual employs a premise first expressed in another book, *The Evolution of Teaching*. That premise is this: We must begin to think of schools as places where two groups learn, students *and* teachers. This premise acknowledges an often overlooked reality. The real places where teachers learn to teach are the schools where they work, not colleges and universities. It is in these workplaces where teachers will spend decades adjusting to the cultures of their schools and adapting to "the way we do things around here" that teachers really learn to teach.

If higher educators, teachers, and supporters of teachers acknowledge this irrefutable reality, then they will see fit to redesign schools for teacher learning, too. In these schools teachers will be empowered to lead their own learning, and it will be thought of as equally intrinsic to the school as student learning is today. In such schools teachers would have a curriculum of their own creation embedded in their daily work. That curriculum would address the general and individual learning needs of teachers at every stage of their careers. The overriding purpose of that curriculum would be the creation of effective teachers.

It is with this premise in mind that aspiring teachers in secondary schools will be best served in their teacher preparation. By designing for themselves a teacher preparation program for secondary school students, aspiring teachers will be given firsthand practice in leading their own learning. At this formative stage, this experience will confirm for them that the schools where they work should, by design, provide them with a career-long process of self and professional realization. Their schools will guide them toward becoming effective teachers.

This leadership of their own learning has long been promised to teachers but never truly given. Now teachers must take control of their profession and make it for themselves. Providing this practice as a formative experience for aspiring teachers in secondary school will, hopefully, create in them the expectation that schools are, indeed, places where teachers design learning for both students and teachers.

FIRSTHAND EXPERIENCE PROVIDES DEEPER LEARNING

This practice for secondary school students in designing their own teacher-preparation learning has a second benefit. It will clarify for them, as prospective teachers, the importance of firsthand experience in the learning process. The famous educator Marion Brady, who emphasized the importance of having students learn not from the secondhand accounts in books but from firsthand experience, has cited the famous philosopher Alfred North Whitehead, who said, "The secondhandedness of the learned world is the secret of its mediocrity."

What this means is that learning is deeper and more authentic when it comes from one's own actions and involvement, not from reading books or listening to lectures and remembering what was in them. This outlook affirms the famous concept advanced by another important educator, John Dewey: people learn best by doing. Thus, this Action Manual hopes to prompt your student to *do* as preparation for being a teacher.

WHAT WILL *STUDENTS* DECIDE TO DO?

This is a daunting question. Your students probably never thought that at their young age they would be called upon to make such decisions or to take action on their decisions. They probably never guessed that the teaching profession would need their help, their leadership. The fact is that it does need their leadership, and they can make a difference NOW.

As your students think about their situation, they should again consider the words of student advocate Edie Holcomb (2007) from her book *Students are Stakeholders, Too!* She explained,

> The American secondary school is the last laboratory in which students can engage in "guided practice" of democracy, citizenship, and individual responsibility. As such, students can and should be true stakeholders in planning and problem solving within their immediate community, the school. (7)

While your students face heavy questions, and the journey does not look easy, it is important to understand that, as Holcomb explained, your students' secondary school is exactly the right place for them to be undertaking these responsibilities. They are in a place where people care about them and will be there to help them as they undertake practicing leadership. If they really care about teaching, it is the right thing to do.

In that context, you and your students are urged to think of it all as an opportunity to grow, and, believe it or not, a way to have fun. Yes, fun. When your students start asking good questions and proposing new ways of doing things, they will be recognized as leaders. That will be fun. They will also become engaged in interesting discussions with thoughtful people. That will be fun. They will likely meet new people and begin to see themselves as a part of an important movement to improve schools. That will be fun, too.

In all of this they will begin to realize that they are important and that they are special. Teachers *are* special people. Their intrinsic motivation to care for the young moves civilization forward. It moves life to a higher place. Understanding this will really be fun. It will brighten their lives, and it will be a great way to begin their careers as teachers.

In guiding your secondary school students to develop their school's teacher preparation programs, you will be helping them to improve their school overall. Having a strong teacher preparation program in your school will get everybody thinking about how to improve teaching and learning for everyone, not just aspiring teachers. By improving your school's teacher preparation program, you and they will make a big contribution to their school.

It is important to be mindful, however, that students responding to the ideas in this book will probably face many different conditions depending on their school. Some schools may have a club or a course or even a larger program for aspiring teachers. Some schools may have no programs or no support at all for aspiring teachers. The recommendations given below will try to help all students regardless of the programs or supports they have right now.

GETTING STARTED

A primary focus of this book has been on teachers being thinkers, decision makers, and leaders who work to build caring communities of learning. As your students consider how they want to express themselves in ACTION, they should again consider the words of Richard and Rebecca Dufour, Robert Eaker, and Thomas Many, authors of *Learning by Doing: A Handbook for Professional Learning Communities at Work* (2006). They have explained, "Most educators acknowledge that our deepest insights and understanding come from action, followed by reflection and the search for improvement" (1–2).

This idea that action leads to insight is the foundation of this Action Manual. It is important to point out that there is a sense in which action has two sets of benefits. There are the external benefits for your school because your students will be improving the school in many ways. There are also the internal benefits. These are harder to describe but have to do with increasing the good stuff in students, things like knowledge, confidence, care, responsibility, compassion, and their all-around goodness as people.

With all of that in mind, the following recommendations will express this desire to actively participate, to gain insight, and to become a better person. That is what will lead to better teachers and better schools.

The Action Manual, then, will be arranged in a way that prompts students to act as members of a learning community: Students as Thinkers; Students Sharing Perspectives and Building Community; and Students as School Innovators and Leaders.

STUDENT AS THINKERS: GET PREPARED FOR CONVERSATIONS WITH OTHERS BY STARTING A CONVERSATION WITH YOURSELF

When your students begin to take action on some ideas they have or some of the recommendations in this book, they will actually be starting their careers as educators. While that may sound a little crazy that they, secondary school students, are starting their work as educators, it is not. When they start asking good questions and making thoughtful proposals, they will be doing the work that educators should do.

Along the way they will find themselves in deep conversations with other students, teachers, and school leaders. The best way to be a positive force as they work with others is to have done a lot of thinking for themselves. The following are questions they might think about. Although no one expects them to come up with final answers to any of them, it is still important to do the thinking. As each student gets involved and starts her or his work as an educator, having thought about these questions and having had a conversation with herself or himself will increase the capacity of each to make a contribution when sharing perspectives with others.

Questions for a Conversation with One's Self

Do I have a theory of how people learn?
How many different ways can people learn?
In what places do people learn?
Am I really learning a lot in school?
Is the game of school a big part of my school's culture, my life?
How much do I play the game of school?
Who is responsible for my learning?
Do I have to go to school to learn?
Does teaching always lead to learning?
In what other ways do people learn?
What are my feelings about teaching, schooling?
What is effective teaching?
Do my teachers need to know what I think about effective teaching?
How do I have fun? How did I have fun as a child?
Can learning be fun? What are some examples?
Should learning be fun?
Can I imagine being eager to get out of the house in the morning to go learn?
Do I find any parts of school fun?
Do I ever teach myself?
Should I be learning more about how to teach myself?
What are the most important things I have learned?
What is the purpose of life? What is the purpose of my life?
Do I ever feel like I have a mission, something I must accomplish?
How does it involve learning?
Do people learn differently at different ages?
Do all people learn in the same way?
How do *I* learn best?
Do I have a certain learning style?
Does school allow me to learn in the ways I learn best?
What influences in life limit how much I learn and grow?
What influences promote and inspire my learning?
Can I identify influences that are holding me back?
Do I ever get in the way of my own growth and learning?
How is learning necessary for a full life?
Can I influence how my teachers teach?
Could I help my teachers do a better job by sharing my ideas with them?
Can I influence what happens at school?
Can I also plan to learn things I love outside of school?
Would it be okay to propose independent or group projects to my teachers?

Do I ever evaluate myself?
Do I ever ask others to give me feedback or evaluate me?
Do I think I have any blind spots about life, learning, myself?
Do I have a personal learning agenda? Should I have one?
Have I ever planned my own learning, or do I just depend on the school?
If I were to start planning my own learning, what would I include?
Who is responsible for my life?
Who's to blame if my life goes bad?
Are students who blindly accept everything the teachers say on the right track?
What are the passive, blind, accepting students missing?
Can I negotiate with all the teachers in my life?
Am I a good teacher? Why?
Even though I am only fifteen (or any young age), why is it important to take ownership of my learning? What is the benefit? What about mistakes?
Do I know anyone who has taken ownership of their learning?
What do I understand about why she or he did it?
If I owned my own learning, how would my life be different?

When students have thought about the questions listed above, they have done some important thinking about teaching. One of the problems we face in the contemporary world is that a lot of people in education have stopped thinking about how people learn and how schools should function.

Instead of thinking about it, they just accept doing things the way they have always been done. They don't bother to imagine new possibilities. But if your students have thought about the questions above, they are better prepared to start questioning the old way and imagining many new possibilities.

YOUR STUDENTS SHARING PERSPECTIVES AND BUILDING COMMUNITY

When your students approach others about starting a conversation about teaching and learning, they will be taking a major step in building community. They will want to let others know that they are aspiring teachers and that they are interested in getting a schoolwide conversation going about teaching and learning. In doing this, they will be behaving like teachers, teachers who believe in listening to students.

As Edie Holcomb has explained, "There must be a place, a space, a structure, to keep engaging, acting on, and broadcasting the student voice" (2007, 7). Their efforts to bring people together to share their voices will help establish the conditions for people to share perspectives and learn together.

A good way to start a conversation is to raise good questions. This shows students are interested in listening to others and are open to new perspectives. People like it when they are invited to contribute. But they should also let people know that their end game is not conversation. It is ACTION. When the conversation reveals opportunities for school improvement, they and their fellow aspiring teachers intend to take some action.

Following are some examples of actions your students could take that would help build community and invite people to share perspectives. The main point is that an important part of a learning community's work is bringing people together to share perspectives and chart the course for teacher learning. Think of the following as a primer list to which your students might add initiatives.

1. Start a formal routine of having students give teachers feedback on their classes and lessons (sort of like class evaluations). There are many ways to do this, and it would probably be best if your school created its own way to facilitate this. Students have great ideas about teaching and learning! (And students should remember that good class evaluations should include what students contribute, too, not just the behavior of the teacher.)
2. Start a Principal's Council for aspiring teachers. This will allow the principal to find out how students think about and experience what is happening in the secondary school. Students can use this book to expand the number of topics discussed and challenge the assumptions underlying twentieth-century schooling.
3. Start a Library/Media Center Council where teachers and students discuss how to support student research and promote the best uses of media for learning *from the student perspective.*
4. Start a Board of Education Council to give *the student perspective* to members of the Board of Education. This will help them make better decisions.
5. Begin involving students in the interviewing of prospective teacher and administrator candidates.
6. Make debating a bigger part of your school's culture. This would mean having students learn the skills of debate and use them in more of their classes. It could also mean holding assemblies or large group affairs where *students debate issues that are important to students.* In some cases this may involve debating school issues and whether or not schools should change.
7. Try to find adults in your school, community, or nearby university who understand the importance of student voice in contributing to a positive school culture and school innovation. Having adults speak up

on your behalf or help students when they speak up will greatly advance the cause of student voice.

Questions to Start a Conversation with Other Students, Teachers, and School Leaders

Once your students find themselves in a meeting with other students and adults, a good way to get started is to raise questions. They might let others in the meeting know that they have been thinking about the following questions as a way of exploring changes schools might make to improve students' engagement and learning.

1. Could students have learning that is more active, less sitting and listening?
2. Could we learn democracy by having more democratic schools?
3. Could we have schools where students and teachers work together?
4. Could we have schools where people really care about each other?
5. Could we have schools where students are listened to?
6. Could we have schools where teachers are the leaders?
7. Could learning at school be more individualized?
8. Could all students learn at their own pace?
9. Could we have learning projects initiated by individuals or groups of students?
10. Could we have learning that is more personally inspired and relevant?
11. Could we have learning that happens in and is about the real world?
12. Could we learn in more ways than reading, writing, and listening in all classes?
13. Could students learn in the ways that suit their unique intelligences?
14. Could we have more community and world service learning?
15. Could we have learning where *students* talk and present?
16. Could we have learning that involves more adults than just the teachers?
17. Could we have learning where every student has a mentor?
18. Could we have learning where students are mentors?
19. Could we have learning in places all over town, not just at the school?
20. Could we get lots of businesses to offer courses so we have lots of choices?

The questions provided above give your students topics to discuss with other students, teachers, and school leaders when they gather as a group. Hopefully, they will have their own questions, too. When they and other aspiring teachers get together for discussions, they will be involved in one of the most important functions of a teacher, communicating with others for the sake of school improvement.

Richard and Rebecca DuFour, Robert Eaker, and Thomas Many have expressed it well in their book *Learning by Doing: A Handbook for Professional Learning Communities at Work* (2006) when they explained,

> Professional learning communities set out to restore and increase the passion of teachers by not only reminding them of the moral purpose of their work, but also by creating the conditions that allow them to do that work successfully. (203)

It is by virtue of people working together as a community that the work of teachers actually gets done. Working together will bring us better schools.

YOUR STUDENTS AS SCHOOL INNOVATORS AND LEADERS

A primary theme in this book is the evolution of teaching and learning. It is about the teaching profession changing in ways that will improve teacher learning and student learning. Thus, this final section is going to prompt your students to act on what needs to be done *to improve students' preparation for teaching while in secondary school.* You and they will likely have some great ideas for improving that preparation.

Students Anticipate Their Happiness as a Developing Teacher

It is important for your students to understand that when they take their first teaching positions after college, it will be at those schools where they will really learn to teach, not in a college program. As new teachers, they will be eager to do what is expected of them, and they will try to fit in. They will look around and begin to do many things the way they see other people doing them. And because they may spend decades in one school, what happens there will tend to override things you have learned in college. In that school, they will learn "the way we do things around here," and that will have a great effect on how they develop as teachers.

Because of this situation, it is important for new teachers to learn to be choosy about the schools where they may decide to teach. It is not easy to assert this kind of choosiness because when they are interviewed and observed as new teachers, they will want to present themselves as cooperative, eager to contribute, and willing to do what is asked of them.

At the same time, because one school may be where most will spend the rest of their careers (twenty-five to forty years), they will want to assess how this school will help them fulfill their potential. Over the course of their careers, *fulfilling their potential will be the biggest factor in feeling satisfied with their career choices and maybe even their lives*. At some point, you may want to refer to my previous book, *The Evolution of Teaching: A Guidebook to the Advancement of Teaching, Teacher Education, and Happier Careers for Early Career Teachers*, and share it with your students as it provides an analysis of what makes teachers happy.

With that in mind, your students will want to ask themselves some questions when they consider schools for the site of their careers. The first question has to do with their philosophy of education. Do they have a philosophy of what is best in schooling and learning? If they are not sure about their philosophy, it is suggested that your students try to write it down and come back to it from time to time. People do develop their philosophies over time. Still, it is important to start thinking about it early.

When they consider a school for their career, they will want to ask themselves whether what is done in that school is consistent with their philosophy about how students and teachers learn best. If they see some consistency, then they will want to consider such schools as sites for their careers. If some don't, the schools in question might only be temporary stops on their career paths.

In further assessing a school, students will want to determine whether the school is really focused on teacher learning at all because many schools are not. Yes, they do provide professional development activities, but they are only occasional, and they tend to lack continuity or be focused on workshops for teaching to the test and raising standardized test scores.

A school that is truly focused on teacher learning will involve teachers in a full array of daily learning that involves action research, lesson study, and collaborative decision making about important aspects of school operations. A school devoted to teacher learning will understand that teachers learn what they do, and doing the intellectual work associated with full participation in school decision making is among the most important of learning opportunities. Ultimately, each of your students will want to ask herself or himself, Do I see that this school will provide me the kind of learning that will help me become the kind of teacher I want to become?

Learning to be choosy about the school where they will situate their careers is an important skill to acquire as they develop into being a teacher. One way to do that now is to have students look at their current secondary school and the kind of professional development opportunities it provides for its teachers. As part of this, you will want to encourage your students to have frank conversations with other teachers about their level of satisfaction with how your school has supported their professional development.

CREATE SCHOOLS THAT CREATE EFFECTIVE TEACHERS

This Action Manual gives you and your students guidance on how to build a teacher preparation program in your secondary school. As you do that, it is important to remember that schools are places where two groups learn, students and teachers. So all schools should have programs for teacher learning throughout their career that help them achieve effectiveness.

Right now in our nation there is a big conversation going on about how to improve student learning. That conversation has zeroed in on one factor in student learning that is more important than any other. That factor is effective teachers. A great deal of research indicates that effective teaching more than any other condition is responsible for improved learning in schools.

Driven by this conclusion, the national conversation on how to improve student learning has now focused on how to create effective teachers. To do this, many education leaders have now placed their attention on improving teacher preparation programs in colleges and universities. But there is a problem with this. The problem is that teachers do not learn to teach in these programs. As explained above, teachers learn to teach in the schools where they work and spend decades adapting to the culture of that school. If those schools are not highly focused on teacher learning, teacher growth is uncertain.

Because we know this to be true, the best way to create effective teachers is to design the schools where teachers' learning actually leads to the creation of effective teachers. Schools should provide teachers a full career of professional learning that, by design, leads to effectiveness. If schools do not have such programs in place, they cannot reasonably be expected to perform at high levels.

THIS IS WHERE YOUR STUDENTS COME IN

This Action Manual is going to provide guidelines for creating a teacher preparation program in your secondary school. That program should be, by design, part of the overall professional learning program that helps teachers achieve full effectiveness.

With this in mind, as your students design their teacher preparation program, they will want to keep asking themselves what it is that teachers need to know and be able to do in order to be effective teachers. When they have decided on this, they can begin to design programs that will help teachers achieve their full potential.

An important part of creating a teacher preparation program will be to coordinate the program with the existing professional learning program for teachers in their school. To properly coordinate with your teachers, they will want to find out what kind of professional learning your teachers do. If your school is a professional development school, they will want to know how the program for secondary school students will blend with the existing program.

School systems generally refer to the learning opportunities provided for teachers as "professional development." Usually a school has a long-term plan of one, two, or more years in place. To start the coordination, students should ask teachers the following questions:

- What process is used in your school to create a professional development plan for the entire school?
- Who is involved?
- What is the plan right now?
- Why do those who created this plan believe its design leads to creating effective teachers?
- Does the plan include special induction activities or events for newer teachers?
- Is our school a professional development school?
- Are the goals for teacher learning coordinated with the school's overall learning goals for students?
- Is the plan made up of occasional outside speakers and workshops?
- Or, are their collaborative learning projects where teachers work together to learn special concepts or skills? For example, do teachers have lesson study where they demonstrate teaching a lesson in front of other teachers, and later the lesson is studied, critiqued, and revised?
- To what extent are students included in teachers' professional learning?
- Are students seen as important partners in helping teachers understand what works and what doesn't work in the eyes of students?
- Would the teachers in your school appreciate the value of including a secondary school student teacher preparation program as part of the overall professional development plan for the school?

Getting your students working with your teachers in this way will be great preparation for being a teacher. It is all about getting people together to share perspectives and talk about how to improve the school. It involves opportunities to collaborate that even college students will not have. Sitting down with their teachers in this way will be an opportunity to demonstrate leadership, and the actual sharing of perspectives could be fun.

BUILDING A TEACHER PREPARATION PROGRAM

What follows is a starter list specifically focused on changes that would improve the preparation of future teachers like yours. Remember, if reading this book is to have any meaning, it must result in your students leading and taking ACTION. Here is a list to help get everyone started.

- Every school should have a future teachers club and/or class. If yours does not, that is where your actions should begin. Bring students and teachers together to discuss how to accomplish this.
- Involve students in preparing the curriculum for this class or activities for the club.
- Invite many teachers to join the club or contribute to the class.
- Affiliate your class or club with a state or national association that has conferences.
- Work with a college or university to create a state association of secondary school students who aspire to teaching if none exists.
- Provide every aspiring teacher with a teacher mentor, someone with whom she or he can talk about being a teacher.
- Teacher mentors should work together to coordinate efforts and activities.
- Aspiring teachers and teacher mentors will do activities together that prepare students for teaching.
- Ask your teachers (during class time) to tell you why they became teachers.
- Ask your teachers to tell you about their own professional learning strategies. How do they work together to learn together?
- Try to coordinate some inclusion of students in teachers' professional learning.
- Have a panel discussion where teachers discuss some of the issues presented in this book.
- Begin to hold regular Instructional Focus Groups that focus on "tell what teachers do that makes you want to learn."
- Communicate with future teachers at other secondary schools.
- Plan a summer event for aspiring teachers, perhaps in coordination with other schools.
- Approach the faculty about investigating student engagement at your school with students as helpers.
- Approach the faculty and school leaders about a schoolwide discussion about the game of school (with fearless student leaders to get people talking honestly).
- Have a discussion with your faculty about the pros and cons of standardized testing.
- Have a discussion with your faculty about the pros and cons of teacher-run schools.
- Provide every prospective teacher with an opportunity to serve as an apprentice to a teacher in your school or an elementary school and allow them to teach sometimes.

- Get involved in your professional development school.
- Have forums and discussions with college students in teacher preparation programs at local colleges and universities.
- Turn your school into a professional development school.
- Start "A Day of Student Voice" where teachers and school leaders will listen to students.
- Start "Days of Dialogue" where teachers and the students in their classes dialogue about issues in learning at school.
- Have discussions among aspiring teachers about the various issues presented in this book.
- Have discussion among aspiring teachers about the teacher preparation programs they are considering and why.

Starting programs like the ones mentioned above will be great preparation for being a teacher. People will begin to see your students as leaders who make things happen. That is what teachers do. When schools need improving, teachers improve them. They do not just keep going through the motions and playing the game of school.

Given all that is being asked of your students in this book, they should know that teachers are very special people. They have very complex jobs that demand enormous intellectual ability and emotional sensitivity. The young people they will be charged with helping in their careers will be extremely diverse in their aspirations and personal needs. Their work will require a high level of commitment.

Unfortunately, there are not enough highly qualified and committed teachers in our nation. Getting more high-quality students to consider teaching is very important work. Hopefully, this book and your efforts have primed them to be thinkers bent on taking action to improve schools.

CONCLUDING WITH CAUTION AND OPTIMISM

This book has focused on two related topics. The first is that as a secondary school student who aspires to teaching, your students are in a unique situation in which they have access to two perspectives, the students' and the teachers'. The second is that these two perspectives need to be shared between the two most important members of any school, the students and the teachers. It is this act of sharing perspectives that builds any community, especially a learning community.

As your students anticipate a career trying to build such a community, they should know that the business of education is very slow to change. Even something that is as apparently as positive as building a learning community can make people nervous. The fact is that educators are very slow to change.

That slowness has been the subject of many books in the last twenty-five years.

So, as they begin to reach out to others and start conversations, they will eventually see that many they will work with will be very cautious about change. When they hear about this book and what the next generation of teachers is proposing, they may begin to show their school blindness and call it all unrealistic. Even the idea of caring communities of learning will be eyed with suspicion primarily because it is outside the experience or vision of most.

As they deal with this school blindness, they should know that most educators have seen many, many change programs come and go, and little has changed. What is important to remember about this, however, is that most of the changes that schools were asked to make in the past came from outside the school. Perhaps the government told schools that they had to change, or the school got some grant money to try change, or there was a short-lived trend in education. Few educators really believed in most of the changes. Then when the government went away or the grant money or the trend ran out, change would stop and people would go back to what they were used to doing.

BELIEVING IN A VISION OF CHANGE

There is a contrast to this, however. Some change has succeeded. Public school teachers have led many of those successes. Some of those have been highlighted in the textboxes following each of the benchmark chapters. Those examples of change succeeded because they were initiated and led by people who had a vision of change *they believed in.* Those people were not being pushed by government, conforming to trends, or being tempted by grant money.

Your students could be like them. After having read their book, they will need to decide what change they believe in. Then, in collaboration with other believers, they can become teachers who lead successful change.

IMAGINATION TRUMPS BLINDNESS

The antidote to school blindness is having a vision and believing in that vision. When your students have a vision of how things can be better, that vision can take them to the place where the reality they want emerges. Remember, although they are few, new schools are emerging, and they are emerging because some committed person or group kept the vision alive and worked to create something new. So, ask your students to imagine . . .

- You are in a secondary school where you get to choose or create courses that really interest you.
- You are in a secondary school where you can build your education around *your* strengths, talents, and aspirations.
- Your teachers take the time to understand you as an individual, your strengths, your weakness, your dreams and aspirations.
- Your schedule might include classroom courses, online courses, group independent study courses, individual independent study courses, local community courses offered by local experts, community college courses, apprenticeships, alternative certificate courses, and more.
- You are in a secondary school where people think learning happens everywhere, not just in classrooms.
- You are in a secondary school where every day you work on solutions for the world's real problems.
- You are in a school that grows food, purifies its own water, provides its own electrical power, and recycles much of its waste.
- You are in a secondary school where students will be asked their opinions about how to improve learning and instruction.
- You are in a secondary school where students will be frequently presenting the outcomes of their projects. It won't just be the teacher up front all of the time.
- Students and teachers are talking about how to change things all of the time. They are talking about how to change the world.
- Students get credit for learning they do outside of school and during the summer.
- Students become teachers to other students when they have the expertise.
- Students who want to become teachers could become apprentices to some classroom teachers in your school.
- Students and teachers are constantly talking about what learning means. It's not just about remembering stuff from the textbooks.
- Students and teachers are out in the community solving problems and creating sustainable change.

Thanks for being a teacher who promises a better future to our future teachers.

References

PREFACE

Davis, J. (2015). *Time and teaching*. Boston: National Center on Time and Learning.
Hattie, J. (2011). *Visible learning for teachers: Maximum impact on learning*. New York: Routledge.
Hattie, J. (2013). *Why are so many of our teachers and schools so successful?* TedX Talks. Accessed at https://www.youtube.com/watch?v=rzwJXUieD0U.

PROLOGUE

Busteed, B. (2014). Make a difference. Show students you care. *Business Journal,* October 9.
Deci, E. (1995). *Why we do what we do.* New York: Penguin Books USA.
Deci, E., & Ryan, R. (1985). *Intrinsic motivation and self-determination in human behavior.* New York: Plenum Press.
Deci, E., & Ryan, R. (2008). Self-determination theory: A macrotheory of human motivation, development, and health. *Canadian Psychology 49*(3), 182–85.
Deming, W. E. (1983). *The new economics.* Cambridge: Massachusetts Institute of Technology, Center for Advanced Engineering Study.
DuFour, R., DuFour, R., Eaker, R., & Many, T. (2006). *Learning by doing: A handbook for professional learning communities at work.* Bloomington, IN: Solution Tree.
DuFour, R., & Fullan, M. (2013). *Cultures built to last: Systematic PLCs at work.* Bloomington, IN: Solution Tree Press.
Esquith, R. (2014). Can't wait for Monday. *Educational Leadership (4)*5, 20.
Farris-Berg, K., Dirkswager, E., & A. Junge. (2012). *Trusting teachers with school success.* New York: Rowman Littlefield Education.
Ingersoll, R. (2012). Beginning teacher induction: What the data tell us. *Education Week,* May 16.
Institute of Education Sciences. (2012). NAEP long-term trends. http://ies.ed.gov/.
MetLife Foundation. (2012). *MetLife survey of the American teacher: Challenges for school leadership.* New York: MetLife, Inc.
Moeny, J. (2015). Don't become a teacher advises award-winner Nancie Atwell. *Education Week Teacher (4)*26.

NCATE. (2010). *Transforming teacher education through clinical practice: A national strategy to prepare effective teachers*. Blue Ribbon Panel on Clinical Preparation and Partnership for Improved Student Learning.

Schlechty, P. C. (2002). *Working on the work: An action plan for teachers, principals, and superintendents*. San Francisco, CA: Jossey-Bass.

Schmoker, M. (2015). It's time to restructure teacher professional development. *Education Week*. October 21.

Senge, P. (1990). *The fifth discipline: The art & practice of the learning organization*. New York: Doubleday.

Senge, P., Cambron-McCabe, N., Lucas, T., Smith, B., Dutton, J., & Kleiner, A. (2000). *Schools that learn: A fifth discipline fieldbook for educators, parents, and everyone who cares about education*. New York: Doubleday.

Sparks, D., & Hirsh, S. (1997). *A new vision for staff development*. Alexandria, VA: ASCD.

Waters, R. (2012). *Secondary students' transitioning from compliance to intentional learning*. (Doctoral Dissertation). Retrieved from UMI ProQuest (Order No: 3504071). Minneapolis, MN: Walden University.

Wenger, E., McDermott, R., & Snyder, W. (2002). *Cultivating communities of practice*. Cambridge, MA: Harvard Business Review Press.

INTRODUCTION

Brown, J. S., & Adler, R. P. (2008). Minds on fire: Open education, the long tail and learning 2.0. *Educause Review*, January/February.

Byrnes, R. S. (2005). To improve high schools, listen to the insights of students. *Education Week*, February 23.

Cook-Sather, A. (2000). Re(in)forming the conversation: Student position, power, and voice in teacher education. *Radical Teacher 64*(Fall), 21–28.

Cook-Sather, A. (2002). Authorizing students' perspectives: Toward trust, dialogue, and change in education. *Educational Researcher 31*(4), 3–14.

Cook-Sather, A. (2006). Change based on what students say: Preparing teachers for a paradoxical model of leadership. *International Journal of Leadership in Education 9*(4), 345–58.

Cushman, K. (2010). *Fires in the mind*. San Francisco, CA: Jossey-Bass.

Damon, W. (2008). *The path to purpose*. New York: Free Press.

DuFour, R., DuFour, R., Eaker, R., & Many, T. (2006). *Learning by doing: A handbook for professional learning communities at work*. Bloomington, IN: Solution Tree.

Fielding, M. (2003). Review of *What Pupils Say* by Andrew Pollard & Pat Triggs. *Journal of Educational Change 4*(1), 38–39.

Hebert, T., & Durham, S. (2008). *High-stakes teaching: Practices that improve learning*. Lanham, MD: Rowman & Littlefield Education.

Holcomb, E. (2007). *Students are stakeholders, too!* Thousand Oakes, CA: Corwin Press.

Joselowsky, F. (2007). Youth engagement, high school reform, and improved learning outcomes: Building systemic approaches for youth engagement. *NASSP Bulletin 91*(3), 257–76.

Mitra, D. L. (2004). The significance of students: Can increasing "student voice" in schools lead to gains in youth development? *Teachers College Record 106*(4), 651–88.

Mitra, D. L. (2008). Amplifying student voice. *Educational Leadership 66*(3), 20–25.

Olson, K. (2009). *Wounded by school: Recapturing the joy of learning and standing up to old school culture*. New York: Teachers College Press.

Rudduck, J. (2002). The 2002 SERA lecture: The transformative potential of consulting young people about teaching, learning and schooling. *Scottish Educational Review 34*(2), 123–37.

Senge, P., Cambron-McCabe, N., Lucas, T., Smith, B., Dutton, J., & Kleiner, A. (2000). *Schools that learn: A fifth discipline fieldbook for educators, parents, and everyone who cares about education*. New York: Doubleday.

Yazzie-Mintz, E. (2009). *Engaging the voices of students: A report on the 2007 & 2008 School Survey of Student Engagement.* Bloomington: Center for Evaluation & Education Policy, Indiana University.

CHAPTER 1

Kelly, F., McCain, T., & Jukes, I. (2009). *Teaching the digital generation: No more cookie-cutter high schools.* Thousand Oaks, CA: Corwin Press.
Senge, P., Cambron-McCabe, N., Lucas, T., Smith, B., Dutton, J., & Kleiner, A. (2000). *Schools that learn: A fifth discipline fieldbook for educators, parents, and everyone who cares about education.* New York: Doubleday.
Waters, R. (2014). *The evolution of teaching: A guidebook to the advancement of teaching, teacher education, and happier careers for early career teachers.* Lanham, MD: Rowman & Littlefield.

CHAPTER 2

Waters, R. (2012). *Secondary students' transitioning from compliance to intentional learning.* (Doctoral Dissertation). Retrieved from UMI ProQuest (Order No: 3504071). Minneapolis, MN: Walden University.

CHAPTER 3

Byrnes, R. S. (2005). To improve high schools, listen to the insights of students. *Education Week*, February 23.
Cook-Sather, A. (2000). Re(in)forming the conversation: Student position, power, and voice in teacher education. *Radical Teacher 64*(Fall), 21–28.
Cook-Sather, A. (2002). Authorizing students' perspectives: Toward trust, dialogue, and change in education. *Educational Researcher 31*(4), 3–14.
Cook-Sather, A. (2006a). "Change based on what students say": Preparing teachers for a paradoxical model of leadership. *International Journal of Leadership in Education 9*(4), 345–58.
Cushman, K. (2010). *Fires in the mind.* San Francisco, CA: Jossey-Bass.
Fielding, M. (2003). Review of *What Pupils Say* by Andrew Pollard & Pat Triggs. *Journal of Educational Change 4*(1), 38–39.
Fielding, M. (2004). Transformative approaches to student voice: Theoretical underpinnings, recalcitrant realities. *British Educational Research Journal 30*(2), 295–311.
Holcomb, E. (2007). *Students are stakeholders, too!* Thousand Oaks, CA: Corwin Press.
Joselowsky, F. (2007). Youth engagement, high school reform, and improved learning outcomes: Building systemic approaches for youth engagement. *NASSP Bulletin 91*(3), 257–76.
Kelly, F., McCain, T., & Jukes, I. (2009). *Teaching the digital generation: No more cookie-cutter high schools.* Thousand Oaks, CA: Corwin Press.
Mitra, D. L. (2004). The significance of students: Can increasing "student voice" in schools lead to gains in youth development? *Teachers College Record 106*(4), 651–88.
Mitra, D. L. (2008). Amplifying student voice. *Educational Leadership 66*(3), 20–25.
Rudduck, J. (2002). The 2002 SERA lecture: The transformative potential of consulting young people about teaching, learning and schooling. *Scottish Educational Review 34*(2), 123–37.
Rudduck, J., & Flutter, J. (2004). *How to improve school giving pupils a voice.* New York: Continuum.
Senge, P., Cambron-McCabe, N., Lucas, T., Smith, B., Dutton, J., & Kleiner, A. (2000). *Schools that learn: A fifth discipline fieldbook for educators, parents, and everyone who cares about education.* New York: Doubleday.

Supovitz, E. H., & Weinbaum, E. H. (2008). *Implementation gap: Understanding reform in high schools.* New York: Teachers College Press.

United States: National Commission on Excellence in Education. (1983) *A nation at risk: The imperative for educational reform: A report to the nation and the Secretary of Education, United States Department of Education (Volume 2).* Ann Arbor: University of Michigan Library.

Yazzie-Mintz, E. (2009). Engaging the voices of students: A report on the 2007 & 2008 high school survey of student engagement. Bloomington: Center for Evaluation & Education Policy, Indiana University.

CHAPTER 4

Black, C. (1997). *Getting out of line: A guide for teachers redefining themselves and their profession.* Thousand Oaks, CA: Corwin Press, Inc.

Brown, J. S., & Adler, R. P. (2008). Minds on fire: Open education, the long tail and learning 2.0. *Educause Review*, January/February.

Busteed, B. (2014). Make a difference. Show students you care. *Business Journal*, October 9.

Chew, J. (2009). Engaging MBA students in problem based learning to foster self-directed learning. *International Journal of Learning 16*(6), 37–49.

Council of Chief State School Officers. (2009). *ESEA reauthorization principles and recommendations: A policy statement of the Council of Chief State School Officers.* Downloaded at http://www.ccsso.org/Documents/2009/ESEA_Task_Force_Policy_Statement_2010.pdf.

Du Four, R. (2010). *The role of professional learning communities in advancing 21st century skills: Rethinking how students learn.* Eds. Bellonca, J. and Brandt, R. Bloomington, IN: Solution Tree.

Jaros, M., & Deakin-Crick, R. (2006). Personalizing learning in the post-mechanical age. *Journal of Curriculum Studies 39*(4), 423–40.

National Governors Association. (2005). Retrieved at http://www.nga.org.

Partnership for 21st Century Skills. (2007). *21st century skills, education & competitiveness: A resource and policy Guide.* http://www.21stcenturyskills.org/index.php?Itemid=120&id=254&option=com_content&task=view.

Scott, S. (2010). Enhancing reflection skills through learning portfolios: An empirical test. *Journal of Management Education 34*(3), 430–40.

Senge, P., Cambron-McCabe, N., Lucas, T., Smith, B., Dutton, J., & Kleiner, A. (2000). *Schools that learn: A fifth discipline fieldbook for educators, parents, and everyone who cares about education.* New York: Doubleday.

CHAPTER 5

Ames, C., & Archer, J. (1988). Achievement goals in the classroom: Students' learning strategies and motivation processes. *Journal of Educational Psychology 80*(3), 260–67.

Bain, K. (2012). *What the best college students do.* Cambridge, MA: Belknap Press.

Blackwell, L. S., Trzensniewski, K. H., & Dweck, C. S. (2007). Implicit theories of intelligence predict achievement across an adolescent transition: A longitudinal study and an intervention. *Child Development 78*(1), 246–63.

Childress, H. (2000). *Landscapes of betrayal, landscapes of joy: Curtisville in the lives of its teenagers.* Albany, NY: State University of New York Press.

Cushman, K. (2010). *Fires in the mind.* San Francisco, CA: Jossey-Bass.

Damon, W. (2008). *The path to purpose.* New York: Free Press.

Dweck. C. S., & Leggett, E. L. (1988). A social cognitive approach to motivation and personality. *Psychological Review 95* (2), 256–73.

Entwistle, N. (1977). Strategies of learning and studying: Recent research findings. *British Journal of Educational Studies 25*(3), 225–38.

Fransson, A. (1977). Qualitative differences in learning: IV. Effects of intrinsic motivation and extrinsic test anxiety on process and outcome. *British Journal of Educational Psychology 47*(3), 244–57.
Gibbs, G., Morgan, A., & Taylor, E. (1982). A review of the research of Ference Maron and the Gotegorg Group: A phenomenological research perspective on learning. *Higher Education, 11*(2), 123-145.
Grant, H., & Dweck, C. S. (2003). Clarifying achievement goals and their impact. *Journal of Personality and Social Psychology 85*(5), 541–53.
Hong, Y., Dweck, C. S., Chiu, C., Lin, D., & Wan, W. (1999). "Implicit theories, attributions, and coping: A meaning system approach," *Journal of Personality and Social Psychology, 77*(3), 588-599.
Littky, D., Garbell, S., *The big picture: Education is everyone's business.* Alexandria, VA: ASCD.
Martin, F., Hounsell, D., & Entwistle, N., eds. (2005). *The experience of learning: Implications for teaching and studying in higher education, 3rd (Internet) ed.* Edinburgh: University of Edinburgh, Centre for Teaching, Learning and Assessment at the University of Edinburgh http://www.tla.ed.ac.uk/resources/Eol.html.
Marton, F., & Saljo, R. (1976). "On qualitative differences in learning: I. Outcomes and process" *British Journal of Educational Psychology, 46*(1), 4-11.
Mueller, C. M., & Dweck, C. S. (1998). Praise for intelligence can undermine children's motivation and performance. *Journal of Personality and Social Psychology 75*(1), 33–52.
Rossum, E. J., & Schenk, S. M. (1984). "The relationship between learning conception, study strategy and learning outcome" *British Journal of Educational Psychology 54*(1), 73-83.
Waters, R. (2014). *The evolution of teaching: A guidebook to the advancement of teaching, teacher education, and happier careers for early career teachers.* Lanham, MD: Rowman & Littlefield.
Zhao, Y. (2012). *World class learners: Educating creative and entrepreneurial students.* Thousand Oaks, CA: Corwin.

CHAPTER 6

Byrnes, R. S. (2005). To improve high schools, listen to the insights of students. *Education Week*, February 23.
Childress, H. (2000). *Landscapes of betrayal, landscapes of joy: Curtisville in the lives of its teenagers.* Albany, NY: State University of New York Press.
Cook-Sather, A. (2002). Authorizing students' perspectives: Toward trust, dialogue, and change in education. *Educational Researcher 31*(4), 3–14.
Cook-Sather, A. (2006). Change based on what students say: Preparing teachers for a
paradoxical model of leadership. *International Journal of Leadership in Education 9*(4), 345–58.
Cushman, K. (2010). *Fires in the mind.* San Francisco, CA: Jossey-Bass.
Damon, W. (2008). *The path to purpose.* New York: Free Press
Holcomb, E. (2007). *Students are stakeholders, too!* Thousand Oaks, CA: Corwin Press.
Joselowsky, F. (2007). Youth engagement, high school reform, and improved learning outcomes: building systemic approaches for youth engagement. *NASSP Bulletin 91*(3), 257–76.
Mitra, D. L. (2004). The significance of students: Can increasing "student voice" in schools lead to gains in youth development? *Teachers College Record 106*(4), 651–88.
Mitra, D. L. (2008). Amplifying student voice. *Educational Leadership 66*(3), 20–25.
Waters, R. (2012). *Secondary students' transitioning from compliance to intentional learning.* (Doctoral Dissertation). Retrieved from UMI ProQuest (Order No: 3504071). Minneapolis, MN: Walden University.
Yazzie-Mintz, E. (2009). Engaging the voices of students: A report on the 2007 & 2008 high school survey of student engagement. Bloomington, IN: Center for Evaluation & Education Policy, Indiana University.

CHAPTER 7

Deci, E. L. (1995). *Why we do what we do.* New York: Penguin Books USA.
Deci, E. L., & Ryan, R. M. (1985). Intrinsic motivation and self-determination in human behavior. New York: Plenum Press.
Deci, E. L., & Ryan, R. M. (2008a). Facilitating optimal motivation and psychological well-being across life's domains. *Canadian Psychology 49*(1), 14–23.
Deci, E. L., & Ryan, R. M. (2008b). Self-determination theory: A macrotheory of human motivation, development, and health. *Canadian Psychology 49*(3), 182–85.
Deci, E., Vallerand, R. J., Pelletier, L. G., & Ryan, R. M. (1991). Motivation in education: The self-determination perspective. *Educational Psychologist 26*(3–4), 325–46.
Goyal, N. (2012). One size does not fit all: A student's assessment of school. Roslyn Heights, NY: Alternative Education Resources Organization.
Hess, F. M., & Manno, B., eds. (2011). *Customized schooling: Beyond whole-school reform.* Cambridge, MA: Harvard University Press.
Kelly, F., McCain, T., & Jukes, I. (2009). *Teaching the digital generation: No more cookie-cutter high schools.* Thousand Oaks, CA: Corwin Press.
Martinez, M., McGrath, D. (2014). *Deeper Learning: How eight innovative public schools are transforming education in the 21st century.* New York: The New Press.
Reeve, J. (2002). Self-determination theory applied to educational settings. In *Handbook of self-determination theory.* Richard R. Ryan & Edward L. Deci, eds. Rochester, NY: The University of Rochester Press.
Ryan, R. M., & Deci, E. L. (2000). Self-determination theory and the facilitation of intrinsic motivation, social development, and well being. *American Psychologist 55*(1), 68–78.
Ryan, R. M., & Deci, E. L. (2006). Self-regulation and the problem of human autonomy: Does psychology need choice, self-determination, and will? *Journal of Personality 74*(6), 1557–85.
Sheehy, K. (2013). Student engagement nosedives in high school. *U.S. News and World Report*, January 16.
Supovitz, E. H., & Weinbaum, E. H. (2008). *Implementation gap: Understanding reform in high schools.* New York: Teachers College Press.

CHAPTER 8

Abelese, V. (Director, Producer), & Congdon, J. (Director). (2009). *Race to nowhere: Transforming education from the ground up.* USA: Reel Link Films.
Ames, C., & Archer, J. (1988). Achievement goals in the classroom: Students' learning strategies and motivation processes. *Journal of Educational Psychology 80*(3), 260–67.
Busteed, B. (2014). Make a difference. Show students you care. *Business Journal,* October 9.
Fredricks, J. A., Blumenfeld, P. C., & Paris, A. H. (2004). School engagement: Potential of the concept, state of the evidence. *Review of Educational Research 74*(1), 59–109.
Northwest Regional Education Library. (2008). *Northwest Education 13*(3) (Spring—Summer): 32–33.
Sheehy, K. (2013). Student engagement nosedives in high school. *U.S. News and World Report*, January 16.
Waters, R. (2012). *Secondary students' transitioning from compliance to intentional learning.* (Doctoral Dissertation). Retrieved from UMI ProQuest (Order No: 3504071). Minneapolis, MN: Walden University.
Yazzie-Mintz, E. (2009). Engaging the voices of students: A report on the 2007 & 2008 High School Survey of Student Engagement. Bloomington: Center for Evaluation & Education Policy, Indiana University.

CHAPTER 9

Childress, H. (2000). *Landscapes of betrayal, landscapes of joy: Curtisville in the lives of its teenagers.* Albany, NY: State University of New York Press.
Cushman, K. (2010). *Fires in the mind.* San Francisco, CA: Jossey-Bass.
Damon, W. (2008). *The path to purpose.* New York: Free Press.
Waters, R. (2012). *Secondary students' transitioning from compliance to intentional learning.* (Doctoral Dissertation). Retrieved from UMI ProQuest (Order No: 3504071). Minneapolis, MN: Walden University.

CHAPTER 10

Bain, K. (2012). *What the best college students do.* Cambridge, MA: Belknap Press.
Busteed, B. (2013). Make a difference. Show students you care. *Business Journal,* October 9.
Deresiewicz, W. (2015). *Excellent Sheep: The miseducation of the American elite and the way to a meaningful life.* New York: Free Press.
Institute of Education Sciences. (2012). NAEP long-term trends. http://ies.ed.gov/.
Scherer, M. (2008). Perspective/The high school scene. *Educational Leadership 65*(8), 7.
Waters, R. (2012). *Secondary students' transitioning from compliance to intentional learning.* (Doctoral Dissertation). Retrieved from UMI ProQuest (Order No: 3504071). Minneapolis, MN: Walden University.
Yazzie-Mintz, E. (2009). Engaging the voices of students: A report on the 2007 & 2008 High School Survey of Student Engagement. Bloomington: Center for Evaluation & Education Policy, Indiana University. Downloaded at http://ceep.indiana.edu/hssse.

CHAPTER 11

Berman, P. (Producer), Sandrich, M. (Director). (1937). *Shall we dance.* USA: RKO Radio Pictures.
Franklin, E. (2013). *Dance imagery for technique and performance.* Champaign, IL: Human Kinetics.
Freed, A. (Producer), Kelly, G., & Donen, S. (Directors). (1952). *Singin' in the rain* [Motion picture]. USA: Metro-Goldwyn-Mayer.
Laurents, A., Ross, H., & Kaye, N. (Producers), Ross, H. (Director). (1977). *The turning point* [Motion picture]. USA: Twentieth Century Fox.
Tharp, T. (2006). *The creative habit: Learn it and use it for life.* New York: Simon & Schuster.

CHAPTER 12

Ames, C., & Archer, J. (1988). Achievement goals in the classroom: Students' learning strategies and motivation processes. *Journal of Educational Psychology 80*(3), 260–67.
Blackwell, L. S., Trzensniewski, K. H., & Dweck, C. S. (2007). Implicit theories of intelligence predict achievement across an adolescent transition: A longitudinal study and an intervention. *Child Development 78*(1), 246–63.
Childress, H. (2000). *Landscapes of betrayal, landscapes of joy: Curtisville in the lives of its teenagers.* Albany: State University of New York Press.
Cushman, K. (2010). *Fires in the mind.* San Francisco, CA: Jossey-Bass.
Damon, W. (2008). *The path to purpose.* New York: Free Press.
Deci, E., Vallerand, R. J., Pelletier, L. G., & Ryan, R. M. (1991). Motivation in education: The self-determination perspective. *Educational Psychologist 26*(3–4), 325–46.

Dweck, C. S., & Leggett, E. L. (1988). A social cognitive approach to motivation and personality. *Psychological Review 95* (2), 256–73.

Grant, H., & Dweck, C. S. (2003). Clarifying achievement goals and their impact. *Journal of Personality and Social Psychology 85*(5), 541–53.

Kelly, F., McCain, T., & Jukes, I. (2009). *Teaching the digital generation: No more cookie-cutter high schools.* Thousand Oaks, CA: Corwin Press.

Mueller, C. M., & Dweck, C. S. (1998). Praise for intelligence can undermine children's motivation and performance. *Journal of Personality and Social Psychology 75*(1), 33–52.

Reeve, J. (2002). Self-determination theory applied to educational settings. In *Handbook of self-determination theory*, Richard R. Ryan & Edward L. Deci, eds. Rochester, NY: The University of Rochester Press.

Ryan, R. M., & Deci, E. L. (2000). Self-determination theory and the facilitation of intrinsic motivation, social development, and well being. *American Psychologist 55*(1), 68–78.

Waters, R. (2012). *Secondary students' transitioning from compliance to intentional learning.* (Doctoral Dissertation). Retrieved from UMI ProQuest (Order No: 3504071). Minneapolis, MN: Walden University.

ACTION MANUAL

DuFour, R., DuFour, R., Eaker, R., & Many, T. (2006) *Learning by doing: A handbook for professional learning communities at work.* Bloomington, IN: Solution Tree.

Holcomb, E. (2007). *Students are stakeholders, too!* Thousand Oaks, CA: Corwin Press.

www.ingramcontent.com/pod-product-compliance
Lightning Source LLC
Chambersburg PA
CBHW021844220426
43663CB00005B/389